INFLUENCE AND
IMPACT

INFLUENCE AND
IMPACT

SUCCESS
BOOKS®
Lake Mary, FL

CONTENTS

CHAPTER 1

TACTICAL EMPATHY: THE GAME THEORY OPTIMUM FOR EFFECTIVE COMMUNICATION

By Chris Voss

Everyone is after the optimum strategy for life. You want to know the tricks to gaining the upper hand. And many people often resort to game theory to work this out. While there's no such thing as a strategy that works every time, what you want is the optimum strategy. Negotiation is similar to this. Nothing can guarantee a win every time. But there is one strategy that'll increase your odds to the optimum success level: tactical empathy.

GAME THEORY STRATEGY FOR HUMAN NATURE

Tactical empathy seems invisible. You employ it, observing the other person's words, absorbing their expression and tone of voice for insights. Then something inside them clicks, like a key that aligns the pins and turns the cylinder, releasing the lock and opening the door.

What exactly happens is a mystery—neither science nor psychology can put an exact point on it. But somewhere in the order of the communication, in the rising and falling momentum, you practiced a form of tactical empathy, and all the parts fell into place. It is astonishing how deeply you can impact a person in a short period of time.

I recently attended a conference in Switzerland for negotiation experts, thinkers, and teachers. There was a gentleman there who billed himself as a cross-cultural negotiation expert, and he was pitching me on how negotiating with Germans is different from negotiating with the Swiss, who are different from the French, the Italians, the Chinese, and so on. He could tell by the look on my face that I wasn't buying any of it. Finally, he blurted out, "Look, everybody just wants to know that you know where they're coming from."

Exactly.

That is the definition of *tactical empathy*. It's the game theory optimum for effective communication in the game of life. It doesn't have anything to do with the cultural aspects of a person being German, Chinese, Spanish, or Puerto Rican. All human beings, under all circumstances, want to know that you understand where they're coming from.

Whether you're a negotiator in a hostage situation or a CEO standing in front of your management team, successful negotiation comes down to a handful of skills, including making sure the other person *feels* understood. This idea seems to be lost today. If you take the time to hear people out and then make them feel heard, you increase your chances of gaining the upper hand.

When someone feels heard, something magical happens. Neurochemicals in the brain are released. *Feeling* heard is a critical binding component to the relationship. It increases trust; it increases the velocity of the collaboration. Even if you don't do what they want, if the person feels totally heard, they're more likely to go along with whatever you're proposing.

It's not a waste of time to listen to someone. When people verbalize their thoughts, they refine their thinking. As the leader, you want to help your people think better. They need to be able to articulate their position, and you're their sounding board. A person might get an unworkable idea, but while it's confined inside their head, it makes sense to them. Many people think better while they talk. So if they don't talk much, they may not be thinking as well as they could be, at least not with precision, because they aren't verbalizing their ideas.

By listening to them, you help them hear themselves. You're going for the moment when they realize, "Now that I've said it out loud, it doesn't really make sense." Or you can paraphrase it back to them: "Here's what you just told me..." And afterward, they say, "Oh, when you put it like that, it doesn't sound right."

You want your employee to say, "My boss didn't always do what I wanted him to do, but he always heard me out. I loved working for that guy."

FBI Agent Turned CEO

I ran a lot of teams at the bureau. With my experience, I thought I was totally prepared to run a company. I had ninety people prepared to deploy overseas in two- or three-person teams, anywhere in the world on any given day, and be able to cover 365 days. I thought I knew running teams. But I still had a thing or two to learn about running a business.

Over the years, here are a few things I've learned:

Not everyone thinks like me.

The first biggest mistake I made was assuming that the people I lead are just like me. There are three default conflict personality types: analyst, accommodator, or assertive. These three types are derivatives of the Thomas-Kilmann Conflict Mode Instrument, which divides people into five types. (The Black Swan team, through our experience and what I learned from my Harvard professors, has built and adjusted these ideas.)

The Black Swan Group has enough anecdotal evidence to support the hypothesis that the entire world splits among these three types evenly—regardless of gender, ethnicity, religion, geography, or anything else. That means that two out of three times it's safe to say you're dealing with a conflict type that is not yours. That means two out of three times, if you're expecting the other person to hear like you or react like you, particularly in conflict, you'll be wrong. Just because I see it one way, two-thirds of the people in the room may not see it the same way. That's not a great success rate.

As an assertive type, I'm a very precise thinker and a very precise listener. It can really throw people off how carefully I listen to them. That also means I'm looking for a very precise answer when I ask a question. I have to warn people, even though it feels very confining, to just give me a straight yes or no. People find that extremely constraining and even frightening because they want to qualify their answer or explain and give context. One-word response? They're horrified. So I've come to learn the hard way that not everybody is an assertive and everybody may not be ready for that concise way of communication.

I shifted from correcting to mentoring.

I've also had the chance to learn what a difference tone makes in regard to how my words land. As an assertive, my natural tone for correction is harsh. It can feel as if you're getting hit in the face with a brick. These days at my company I'm focusing very much on taking a mentoring approach with employees. In my approach and my tone this mindset will soften me significantly so my words are more likely to land. I will even state, "I'm mentoring you right now."

I also have an appreciation of how harsh it is to get corrected by me. If I've made the mistake of correcting a person, then I follow up two or three times that same day to make sure the residual impact of that encounter is not embedded and festering.

A lot of leaders out there won't do that. They just figure the person they were harsh with can lick their wounds and move on or leave, because that's what they did when they were coming up through the ranks. They forget how painful it felt. Now they're on the other side of it, and they've healed up, but it was probably pretty devastating to them in the moment. And even though they got over it, which everybody ultimately has to do, it may not have been the most effective way to go about a resolution. Considering this hypothesis, you have to ask, "Is your way the most effective way for that person who got corrected?"

The more you mentor, the less you'll need to correct, which will save a lot of time. Having said that, there are moments when you'll have to correct someone.

Be careful.

If you've been mentoring them for a while, your correction is going to land far more abruptly because there will be a contrast in the way you're speaking to them. Suddenly, it's not warm and fuzzy, and that difference will jump out to them. It's clear this is important, and at the same time you will need extra follow-up to make sure they don't spiral downward.

You know the old phrase "When you're good with a hammer, everything looks like a nail." *Rarely* is it actually a nail.

When I have to correct someone, I'll throw out, "I've got to mentor you a little bit," so they're ready when it comes and they feel less beat up on.

I write things down by hand.

I hate multitasking. And it's been demonstrated over and over again that it makes you a perpetual C student in comparison with what you're actually capable of.

Typing is effectively multitasking times four, or six, or ten, depending on how many fingers you use to type. You're sending messages to all different points of the hand, and each synaptic neural connection is doing a different job simultaneously. You dilute your focus. With handwriting, you're taking all the mental energy into one hand, and you're focusing it down to one point, which causes, in my view, five times the amount of focus. Handwriting is more effective in terms of retention and even creativity. Statistically, I've heard you absorb 40 percent more information when you write it down.

I forgot what it was like when I was still learning.

When a leader comes to a conclusion, we forget how long we've thought about it. We might get an epiphany overnight, or while we're having coffee, or on the drive in the morning. The answer is clear. We forget how long we've had to think about it, even subconsciously. This idea has been living in our head for a while. Reaching that conclusion took the amount of experience, insight, acumen, and perspective we have. And so, because it's so utterly clear to us in a moment, we expect it to be utterly clear to other people when we articulate it. We don't think about how long it took us to reach that point.

When we were working on the book *Never Split the Difference* with Tahl Raz, my son Brandon and I would explain things to Tahl that we thought were crystal clear. Brandon and I are very much like-minded on how we communicate. But Tahl would be like, "Wait, you forgot what it's like not to know this stuff. This all seems really obvious to you guys, but what you just said makes no sense to somebody who doesn't know."

I think leaders forget what it was like to not know, to remember a time when they were at an earlier level of experience, age, or point on the journey. Nowadays, leaders just want to tell people to save them time and effort because it seems so obvious. Well, it ain't. Slow it down and remember, not everyone is as far down the road as you are.

If we disagree, I get to make the mistake.

There has to be a tacit agreement as to who gets to make the mistake when two people disagree on the best path forward. I talk to people who work with me and for me a lot. I'll tell them, "If we've heard each other out and we still disagree, since I'm going to pay for the mistake anyway, then I get to be the one who makes the mistake." This is basically an up-front negotiation and prepares people for when you don't do what they think you ought to do.

I listened to an interview Lex Fridman did with Jeff Bezos. Jeff was telling his employees to do exactly what he told them to do...unless they had a better way. But understand that *better* is not a synonym for *different*. If you want to do it your way because you're more comfortable with it or because it's worked for you in the past, that's just different, not better. As a leader, I'm happy to be overruled if you can show me a better way to get to where I want to go.

I've seen this play out even with the most control-freak leaders. I knew a leader in the FBI who was absolutely not open to hearing a different way to get where he wanted to go and wanted to approve everything before it was implemented. He was dead set on his way. Even the people who liked him didn't like working for him. One day an FBI agent came along and effectively overruled him in front of a large group of people. He just said, "John, we're not doing it like that." And since it was in front of a group, and because John had liked this guy a lot already, he chuckled and said, "OK, how are we going to do it?" The agent laid out a different course of action that got John where he wanted to go but faster. And John loved it.

From that point on John sang this agent's praises. That agent could do no wrong, because he demonstrated that he understood where John wanted to go and he figured out a better way to get there.

Hire the good people under your nose.

I've had to adapt the way I hire team members because using typical hiring agencies wasn't bringing me the kind of employees I needed. The first clue was when I realized a high turnover rate for assistants. There might have been several reasons for this, not the least of which was a person in this role may get a lot of correction from me, which is often going to feel harsh. Since some of these previous employees were virtual, that left no time to shift from correcting to mentoring. With no in-person downtime as a team, it leads to burnout and resignations.

But something else was going on—some flaw in the typical hiring process. Black Swan is a high-performance company. When we followed the lead of a recruiting service, we'd be lucky to get a B player, and mostly we got C players. We can't tolerate low-level performers.

I started looking for people who are top performers right under my nose—the people who I encounter in person, in the city where I live, who impress me with their service. A couple of examples: I'm in and out of The UPS Store, and I noticed a young man who worked there who seemed organized and was a good problem solver. He had a great demeanor, even with demanding customers. The other employees didn't always know where my packages were, but if he was working that day, he always knew where to find them. He also remembered my name. One day I took the guy off to the side and asked him what he was making and what ambitions he had for his life. He told me what he made and that he eventually wanted to go to film school.

"Look, let me bring you onto my team. I'll pay you more than you're making right now, and we've got a ton of video to shoot and produce for our training and our YouTube channel." I told him when he's ready to pursue his film career, he'll do it with the experience of having worked on a lot of video and at a respected company. We brought him on board, and it's worked out great.

I also hired a young lady from the Apple Store who impressed me. She ultimately wants to be in law enforcement, but I asked her to come to my company, and whenever I saw the chance, I'd expose her to ideas about working in law enforcement, because we've got a bunch of people in the company who are retired law enforcement. She'd have the chance to talk to them and get their guidance.

When I paid attention to the people right under my nose, I started bringing on employees who lasted longer and were a better fit with the company's values.

All these lessons have made me a better team player and a better people manager. Managing a team can carve off the rough edges in a leader. Some of what I've learned as a CEO has been practical, and some of it came from what I already knew. What never changed, and what is present on some level anytime I communicate, is how I practice empathy to achieve the desired outcome.

EMPATHY IS NOT WEAKNESS

Empathy doesn't have a downside. When you let the other person know you understand where they're coming from, you build an invisible connection of trust that leads to the best chance of success. It's the game theory optimum.

Leading with empathy doesn't mean you're weak or a pushover. You don't compromise your position. Empathy is not sympathy. With sympathy, you're dragged into somebody else's quicksand. Emotions get involved. Leaders are horrified they'll appear as if they're weak, a pushover, or not the expert. But it is possible to be soft-spoken and even show kindness but still not give in.

These days I'm seeing more and more stories of female leaders finding success while still maintaining their femininity. Up until very recently a woman had to become one of the guys to be successful in business. In many ways that myth is still out there. But I've watched female leaders—such as Camille Vasquez, who was the trial attorney in the Johnny Depp/Amber Heard defamation trial—model a leadership style that is uncompromising, empathetic, and feminine. I see her as one of many emerging female leaders who are achieving a higher level of success than their male counterparts.

We impact and influence the people around us by staying students of human nature. It is energizing to see new leaders who are building an invisible connection of trust because they listened closely to the people they work for and with, and made sure the people felt heard. When we hire people with the right core values and mentor them as they develop, we grow the pool of people we want to collaborate with. We build leaders who spark creative solutions and who raise the collective intelligence in a room.

Ultimately, the master of the game ends up being the one who most quickly figures out the rules of the dynamic unfolding between you and your counterpart. Be agile as you gather information. Stay creative with your problem-solving. And whatever you do, don't forget that no strategy is consistently more effective in gaining a win than tactical empathy.

About Chris

Chris Voss is the best-selling author of *Never Split the Difference*, a former lead international FBI kidnapping negotiator, and the CEO and founder of The Black Swan Group.

During his twenty-four-year career with the FBI, Chris served as the FBI's hostage negotiation representative for the National Security Council's Hostage Working Group and has represented the US at two international conferences. He's been recognized for a number of awards, including the Attorney General's Award, and the FBI Agents Association Award for Distinguished and Exemplary Service. He has received negotiation training from the FBI, Scotland Yard, and Harvard Law School.

Since retiring from the FBI, Chris has earned his master's in public administration from Harvard University and taught at a number of esteemed institutions, including the University of Southern California Marshall School of Business, Georgetown University, Harvard University, Northwestern University, the IMD Business School in Lausanne, Switzerland, and the Goethe Business School in Frankfurt, Germany.

Following the success of his book *Never Split the Difference*, Chris coauthored a book with real estate guru Steve Shull, *The Full Fee Agent*, which provides practical and skillful negotiation techniques for real estate agents—both experienced and expert. Chris has been featured on podcasts and media outlets such as *Time* magazine, CNN, CNBC, the Lex Fridman podcast Inc., and others.

His company, The Black Swan Group, established in 2008, aims at providing negotiation coaching for professionals all over the world through corporate and individual coaching, as well as live events.

When he isn't coaching or giving keynote speeches, Chris is passionate about learning, working out, reading, and spending time with his family. He currently lives in Las Vegas.

To connect with Chris and his company, you can go to blackswanltd.com. You can also follow him on LinkedIn and Instagram.

CHAPTER 2

FROM EMIGRANT TO CEO

A Journey of Courage, Data, and Purpose

By Julia Bardmesser

"**D**o you understand," he asked, "you may never see Baba Tanya again?"

I knew my father-in-law was just trying to make sure I fully understood the irrevocability of our decision, but his comment came across as cold and uncaring, and I held it against him for years.

Baba Tanya was my beloved grandmother, and as my then husband and I had decided to emigrate to America, I, even then a student of history, knew that the iron curtain could come down again at any time without warning and I would never see my family again.

What do I remember of our journey? Not much, just moments in time, like old photographs or fragments of staticky home movies.

I remember the farewell circle of my friends and relatives on a platform in the Kyiv railway station. My mom was in that circle too, and neither one of us cried, though both of us were very aware that there were no guarantees we'd ever see each other again. Oddly, the circle felt festive, a kind of bon voyage party with all of us naively choosing to believe that everything would turn out well and that the others would follow us to America as soon as they could.

I remember standing just inside the door of the Vienna-bound train in Chop and looking at my father. The train wasn't moving yet, but its tracks crossed the border, and our car was sitting on the other side. I could see my dad standing behind the invisible line, closely watched by border police. We were still so close, yet already vastly apart. It was after midnight and bitterly, relentlessly cold, and he was wearing dress shoes. I saw him dance a bit to keep his feet from freezing. But he stayed, unwilling to abandon the platform for the warmth of the station until the train pulled away and we couldn't see each other anymore.

Today, thirty-three years later, I am the CEO of Data4Real, a strategic advisory company providing trusted, unbiased, reality-based advice to organizations on a mission to create maximum value from data, AI, and digital assets.

I've spent the last thirty years growing a data-centric career in the financial industry, and I have served in leadership positions in some of the most well-known financial institutions in the world.

But back then, I was a young woman—a bit scared but mostly hopeful—embarking on the greatest journey of my life with no resources other than my brain and my courage.

Both courage and hopefulness came from my family, mostly from Baba Tanya.

Baba Tanya, my grandma, was a scientist. She was born in 1918. She worked as a materials research scientist all her life, but at fifty years old, she finished her dissertation, got her PhD, and became a head of a large research team in one of the premier material science institutes in Kiev.

She had high-level security clearance and worked with the Soviet Union space and weapons program. My grandmother knew about Chernobyl before all the civilians did—she was asked about the best materials to put on top of the reactor to dampen the radiation.

We spent a lot of time together, especially in the summer, in monthlong vacations in resort towns near Riga, Latvia. We walked, we talked, we read, we entertained her science colleagues, and I absorbed her confidence and her belief that everything is possible, always.

Year in and year out I remember sitting down for dinners she hosted for her colleagues across the entire Soviet Union. They were brilliant men (and yes, except for my grandma, they were all men), and I loved hanging out with them. That early entry into such a community of such intellect and depth of knowledge, not to mention power, served me well throughout my career.

I don't get intimidated easily.

That's a gift that would come in handy as I worked my way up to senior-leadership positions in what was largely a male-dominated financial-services industry.

Another thing from my upbringing that turned out to be massively useful, especially as I moved into the data-management space, is caring deeply about accuracy and truthfulness. The Soviet Union propaganda had neither, so as I moved into my new life, I wanted to do everything I could for this to be different.

IF YOU WANT TO HAVE INFLUENCE, DON'T BE A CLOISTERED NUN

I had just been promoted to manage a data team at a financial company. I was excited! I knew the challenges the company was facing and was confident I could make a difference.

I happily walked into the building and made my way over to introduce myself to a colleague.

She looked at me and said, "I feel so sorry for you."

Huh? Where were the congratulations?

She went on, "I feel sorry for you because data is like electricity—nobody notices it unless it's not working. It's only when you flip the switch and nothing happens that people realize its importance."

Even now, many years later, in the data-is-the-new-oil and AI era, this statement rings uncomfortably true.

Why do data teams go unrecognized? It's simple, really. Change is disruptive, and humans, by nature, are resistant to it. Data teams challenge the status quo, question long-held beliefs, and push boundaries. Our recommendations are met with skepticism, and our findings are often massively inconvenient.

But the biggest reason is that we spend most of our time hidden behind our computers and working through other teams.

As I took over yet another data team a few years later, I saw the same dynamic and I looked for something that would help both my team and the broader business and IT community break this pattern.

Luckily, the pictures from my recent food tour to Seville helped. I loved Seville! It was gorgeous, boasting a cathedral that is huge and ethereal at the same time, oranges hanging on the trees, and the food was incredible! I told my team a story...

One day we went on a food tour of the city. Our group was buzzing about a particular cookie that was on our list of must-haves, but the excitement wasn't just for the cookies. The chatter was about the fact that the cookies were made by cloistered nuns who lived behind the monastery walls right in the middle of the city but were never seen. Cloistered nuns cannot see or be seen by the outsiders, but they needed additional income and so were selling cookies based on the centuries-old recipe.

How were we going to buy cookies from someone we weren't allowed to see or speak to?

We went into the courtyard surrounded by the stone walls and saw the most ingenious contraption to sell a cookie.

There was a window in the stone wall, and in that window there was a tall lazy Susan. We put some money in it and turned it, and a moment later—a box of cookies!

The cookies were great, and after we polished them off, we spent some time wondering whether there were other foods they made and about what life behind that stone wall might be like.

This kind of mystery was charming in a food tour, but for a data team—not so much!

I shared this story (and the picture) with my team and the rest

24

of the organization. It was painfully obvious that no other division in the organization had any idea why we did what we did, how to leverage us and how our work improved business operations. We were invisible, cloistered nuns!

You cannot have any influence if people don't know you exist, or if they know you exist but they don't know *why*.

Ditch the lazy Susan, come out from behind the stone wall and proudly share not just the cookies but why the organization needs them.

ANCIENT SUMERIAN BUSINESS SECRETS

The Sumerians were a **people of southern Mesopotamia** who lived between 4100 and 1750 BCE.

They are credited with being responsible for the first-ever recorded instances of writing.

They are called the Sumerian Tablets. These stone tablets are carved with ancient Sumerian text, and when they were discovered, scientists, archaeologists, and academics were beside themselves with anticipation.

Could these ancient stone scrolls hold the key to the meaning of life? Would they reveal religious epiphanies?

No.

What disappointed translators discovered was that the Sumerian Tablets were nothing more than a list of products. It was the first-ever inventory! Instead of life-changing, sacred guidance, they had before them a list of transactions, administrative concerns, and records of purchases. In essence, they revealed the first-ever recorded instance of *data*!

The value of data was perhaps more understood thousands of years ago than it is today.

What I have seen time and time again is that the business divisions of organizations have trouble describing their offerings, they have trouble discerning how their offerings fit into market, and they struggle to read the data that answers those questions.

And we all know what happens when something is complicated—we give up and walk away.

I have seen brilliant executives throw their hands up in exasperation and make decisions based on their gut feelings because they didn't have the data or, even worse, they had it but didn't trust it.

That's why I made it a practice to train my teams to speak the language of their business counterparts.

It's tempting when you're persuading someone to resort to impressing them with your knowledge, throwing in complex industry jargon and showing off your expertise.

But that's often counterproductive.

I taught my team to stop talking technology and instead explain in plain terms how the findings would increase or decrease profit, and to offer recommendations in a way that would make sense to anyone regardless of their level of understanding of data.

The most persuasive communication is simple to understand and directly tied to the outcome the other party wants.

No one is interested in diving into the inner workings of a clock. They just want to know what time it is!

Leave out the details and go *simple*.

DATA RICH, INSIGHT POOR

In any negotiation or business interaction that requires two sides to come together, it's not uncommon for the parties to have every bit of information they need to make a sound decision but no clue how to glean meaningful value from that information.

That's what we call being data rich but insight poor.

We have the facts, but our failure to understand the facts brings everything to a screeching halt.

How can anyone change or take corrective action if they can't make sense of the actionable conclusion the facts are presenting?

This is a call to *lead*.

If you find that the person or team that you're trying to persuade just isn't understanding the facts, don't view it as a stalemate but rather an invitation. You are being invited to lead the conversation and bridge the gap for them!

I tell my teams all the time to remember that the role of a data officer or data analytics officer is not a technology role.

It's a change-management job.

The role isn't just to own the data strategy; it's to make the *other* side own it.

No matter what industry you're in, this shift in perspective is essential to master persuasive communication—the other party should not be seen as just a stakeholder in the negotiation but rather as its owner.

Ask questions such as:

What are your priorities for this year?

What are you working on?

What frustrates and challenges you the most?

When you understand what they are trying to achieve and the obstacles standing in their way, you are in a much better position to explain how your point of view supports their desires and solves their fears.

Don't just present your facts.

Instead, provide insight into how those facts ultimately, with time and collaboration, will culminate in something even greater than they are imagining right now.

YOUR MOST PERSUASIVE TOOL IS PURPOSE

Baba Tanya ultimately made her way to the United States a few years after me. I loved being able to just lift the phone and talk to her every day.

Over the years, she remained sharp, solving crossword puzzles and asking my daughter questions about her science courses in school. I never saw the typical cognitive issues that come with age. Yet I watched her shrink, both physically and metaphorically.

In Russia my grandma was not your typical cookie-baking,

sweater-knitting baba. She was writing books, leading research teams, planning adventures, and following her insatiable curiosity!

The woman who was so alive and revered in her home country was small and invisible in the United States. I would watch her interact with a store clerk and wonder if he had any idea this little old woman that he was bartering with used to be one of the most brilliant and respected scientific minds in the Soviet Union!

This change in rank seemed to cause a quick deterioration.

It made me wonder, "Was it really geography that robbed her of wielding influence? Or had she simply disconnected from her purpose, the move being so monumental and the change so great that she could no longer connect to her own brilliance?"

It happens to all of us at some point.

We find ourselves in a new place, or with a new team, or in a room we feel unqualified to be in, and we shrink.

What I have found time and time again is that if I just reconnect to my inherent purpose, courage follows.

Persuasion can be intimidating, but purpose will always shine brighter than credentials.

Remember that the next time you are in a room of people with big titles, or finding your way in a new country, or advocating for a cause that's close to your heart.

You belong there. Your goal is valid. And your gifts are needed.

Baba Tanya died in Brooklyn at the age of ninety-nine.

The influence and impact she had on my life are hard to put into words, but I'll try.

Because of her I was brave.

Because of her I was able to do work that inspired me and make the impact *I* wanted to make in this world.

Because of her I am sitting here with a lifetime of adventures and wisdom under my belt, telling you these stories.

If you want to have influence and make an impact, get out front; lead productive, respectful conversations; look for ways to provide insights that are meaningful to the other party; and if they still can't hear you?

Return to your purpose.

It will always tell you exactly what to do next.

About Julia

Julia Bardmesser is the founder and CEO of Data4Real, a strategic advisory firm that provides trusted, unbiased, and reality-based advice to executive leaders aiming to unlock the maximum value from their data, digital, and AI assets.

Julia is a global executive in AI, data analytics, and risk management. She is an expert in business value-aligned tech transformation, from vision and strategy through road map and execution. Her specialization lies in modernizing processes for strategic growth and operational efficiency throughout the business lifecycle. With over twenty years' experience, Julia is an industry-recognized, award-winning thought leader in data-driven digital transformation. Her work has enabled business growth, innovation, and agility in financial services companies such as Voya Financial, Deutsche Bank, and Citigroup.

In her previous role as the senior vice president, head of data, architecture, and customer relationship management (CRM) technology at Voya Financial, she spearheaded Voya's data, cloud, and analytics transformation by harnessing enterprise data and technology capabilities. Her strategic initiatives facilitated innovation, agility, and rapid market responsiveness by unlocking key insights from proprietary data.

Throughout her career Julia has been a trailblazer in the financial industry. She has held leadership positions at prominent institutions such as Citi, FINRA, Freddie Mac, Thomson Financial Services, Bear Stearns, and Bloomberg LP.

Beyond her corporate achievements, Julia is an active participant in the technology start-up ecosystem. She serves on the advisory boards of several start-ups: The Medici Project, Polymer, and Fluree.

Her contributions have been recognized globally.

She has been named to the engatica 2023 list of the World's Top 200 Business and Technology Innovators.

She is the recipient of the prestigious 2022 WLDA Changemaker in AI award.

Julia has been named on CDO Magazine's List of Global Data Power Women three consecutive years, highlighting her impact on the data and analytics field.

Top 150 Business Transformation Leaders by Constellation Research

(2019): Her visionary leadership earned her a place among the top transformational leaders.

Best Data Management Practitioner by A-Team Data Management Insight (2017): Julia's commitment to excellence was acknowledged through this esteemed award.

Additionally, she is a founding member of Women Leaders in Data and Artificial Intelligence (WLDA), where she contributes to fostering diversity and innovation.

As a sought-after speaker and mentor, Julia shares her expertise with the broader community. Julia's dedication to advancing the field of data and analytics is evident through her published contributions in CDO Magazine.

She holds a master of arts in economics from New York University.

CONNECT WITH JULIA:

LinkedIn: www.linkedin.com/in/julia-bardmesser
Website: www.data4real.com

CHAPTER 3

THE TIDES OF RESOLVE

By Mark Scribner

"I'm going to die."

The frigid embrace of the English Channel enveloped me as I bobbed up and down in the pitch-black abyss. The boat was nowhere to be found, and every bit of light had been swallowed by the clouds. I was completely alone, battling fifteen-foot waves and the relentless sting of the jellyfish.

A current of emotions surged through me, a cocktail blend of adrenaline and panic.

"I can't die here."

Images of my family flashed through my mind. In my head I saw my kids. I saw my mom, whose death had prompted this charity swim.

On one shoulder sat the devil.

"Give up. It's over."

On the other shoulder, an angel.

"Stay alive. Keep swimming. You can do this."

In that moment of inner debate, the channel stretching for miles in front of me, I knew that the only thing that could save me was to get control of my own mind.

Fighting extreme exhaustion and surrounded by blackness, disorientation threatened to overtake me.

I needed to find equilibrium, and *fast*.

It wasn't my first endurance event, but it was the first time I felt as if I was fighting for my life. It's one thing to push your body and achieve a personal best, but waging war against an angry black ocean requires a level of mental toughness most people never have to tap into.

But could!

Over the years, I have learned that absolutely anything is possible when you learn to train your brain to search for and achieve equilibrium.

My entrepreneurial odyssey commenced at the tender age of twenty-two. In the nascent stages, my focus was set on how a business carves out a market niche, delivers value, and ensures longevity.

In 1986, amid the tumult of a stock market crash, I aspired to be a stockbroker. Bob, the hiring manager, candidly assessed that I lacked the sartorial flair, the prestigious academic pedigree, and the mathematical prowess deemed essential for capital markets.

He suggested plumbing as a more fitting pursuit.

Undeterred, I met his gaze, extended a handshake, and with a defiant smile I silently vowed to prove him wrong.

Fast-forward four years—I not only entered but conquered Wall Street, claiming Bob's very office as my own. His skepticism inadvertently fueled my resolve to thrive in the industry.

Throughout my career, my journey has been enriched by a nationally syndicated podcast, interactions with thought leaders at TEDx Beacon Hill, MIT, and a diverse client base. These experiences have positioned me at the epicenter of innovation, allowing me to ask pivotal questions and emerge as a thought leader guiding my clients to unlock their enterprise value.

The search for equilibrium that saved my life in the English Channel is the same guiding force that has helped me leverage those opportunities and build a hugely successful career.

In business, mutual benefit is the linchpin of sustained collaboration. The ideal equilibrium—be it fifty-fifty or sixty-forty—varies across industries. However, when the scales tip too far, discord ensues. I've witnessed the pitfalls of unsustainable practices where gross margins, contracts, or negotiations favor only one party.

It isn't pretty.

My career has been a testament to the relentless pursuit of *equitable balance*, ensuring that value and fairness are omnipresent in every business interaction and relationship.

Equity is a constant endeavor.

In any endurance event, the search for balance starts with visualizing the best possible outcome. As obstacles are thrown into your path, it's easy to start making excuses, become frantic, and consider giving up.

The best thing to do in those moments is negotiate with yourself.

Too often in business we take an us-against-them approach. The best athletes and the best negotiators in the world know that the true fight is you against you.

Instead of focusing on the miles ahead, persuade yourself to stick it out five more minutes. Then reevaluate. The same is true in business interactions. The most successful outcomes happen one step at a time. When the other party is challenging you, let go of the global result you're looking for, and drill it down to minutes. Stay in the race. Ask questions to dig for the truth.

And always strive for equilibrium.

When Equal Isn't Equal

Equilibrium is a delicate dance between internal and external factors. It requires proactive and ongoing attention and the ability to adapt at a moment's notice.

In any negotiation, striving for and maintaining equilibrium is key in keeping a conversation flowing and moving in the right direction.

At the core, it's the presence of value. Everyone involved has to feel as if they are receiving value in return for the time and money they're giving.

There's a quote that reads that "Price is only an issue in the absence of value."

If you'd like some evidence of that quote in action, take a trip to Disney World.

A week at Disney can cost anywhere from $7,000–20,000. A sweatshirt is $100. A lollipop is $25.

And yet fifty million people visit every year and don't bat an eye at the price tag, and that's because Disney has cracked the code on how to make visitors feel that they are receiving massive value.

They personalize your experience.

They pay close attention to detail.

They offer upgrade options that open the door to shorter lines and other sought-after conveniences.

Hard-working Americans save for years to spend a week plowing through crowds and waiting in line in exchange for a few magical moments.

Equal? Maybe not. Worth it? Just ask the kids.

The perceived value is high enough that as soon as people get home, they start saving to go back.

It isn't just Disney. The Ritz-Carlton has also perfected the art of service. My mother was a nurse who worked three jobs for thirteen years and delivered exceptionally compassionate service. In fact, watching her over the years opened my eyes to the importance of focusing on kindness and service no matter where I was or whom I was with.

As I grew in my career, I found that marrying happiness with business was key to a high perceived value and successful negotiations.

I can't always promise that a contract will be equal, but I can promise that it will be fair and that the other party will feel seen and taken care of and receive value.

I can also confidently predict that everything will change. The balance we work so hard to establish will be disrupted by market volatility, changes in customer behavior, or unexpected glitches in supply chains.

Suddenly, we have to adjust our strategy or reallocate resources.

Similarly, in life, equilibrium can be disrupted by relationship changes, health concerns, and unexpected curveballs.

I can tell you from my experience in Ironman competitions

that things will go wrong. Muscles will detach, tendons will break, and in those moments, the finish line isn't the focus. The focus must be restoring balance.

The same is true in business negotiations. Sometimes achieving equilibrium may require sacrificing short-term gains for long-term stability, and the goal has to shift.

Resilience and adaptability are key.

STEPS TO ACHIEVING HARMONY

A strong, successful negotiator knows that the key to winning is not to get the other side to lose; it's to get the other side to feel that your proposal adds value and works to meet their needs.

That said, the first step in achieving equilibrium is to know what it looks like for all participants.

What does the other side need to feel balanced?

Remember, everyone at the table is trying to get the most out of the transaction, but they are not trying to get the most overall, just the most *they* can get.

It's a subtle difference but an important one.

If your goal is to get more than everyone, you've upset the balance.

If your goal is to get the other party as much as possible while maintaining harmony on your end, you're moving in the right direction.

Find their perceived gaps in value, and fill them.

The second step is to consider how you will measure when equilibrium has been achieved.

What data points and feedback are *you* looking for? Let's say you're leading a real estate transaction. What does a perfect transaction look like? What would need to happen for everyone to walk away feeling as though they got a great deal? And it isn't just about the money. Do the buyer and seller feel served? Did they get white-glove service? Did they maybe spend more than they planned to but get more than they originally asked for?

Raising the perceived value for all involved is about offering authentic solutions in service to harmony and the collective good.

The third, and perhaps most important, step in achieving equilibrium is to be willing to modify all plans and strategies to meet current models and changing needs.

A lot of business leaders make the mistake of thinking that modifying means compromise. Compromise, by nature, usually signifies that both sides are making concessions and giving something up.

But in the context of establishing equilibrium, the idea isn't to give something up but to adjust strategies and conditions, paving *multiple* paths to success.

Picture two ships, each sailing on a tumultuous sea, each manned by two captains determined to reach their destination.

One captain, driven by ambition, charges ahead at full speed.

The other, more prone to caution, sails slowly and carefully, mindful of the treacherous waves.

Both ships continue to encounter challenges that upset their course. The speeding ship pushes headlong into waves, risking damage. The cautious captain avoids danger but is drastically behind his projected timeline for reaching port.

Neither is likely to be successful unless they establish balance.

The ambitious captain would be wise to temper his drive for speed and keep his boat intact. The cautious captain needs to realize that progress requires a willingness to take a few calculated risks.

With those vastly different adjustments, both will reach port unscathed and hopefully on time.

Business negotiations also require a delicate dance between ambition and caution, between change and tradition. By striking this balance, we can navigate uncharted waters to unprecedented innovation.

Right now we are experiencing a call to adapt, thanks to the rapid introduction of artificial intelligence.

AI is one of the most disruptive adaptations in human history, rivaling the massive changes faced by society during the industrial revolution.

Back then, society was completely reshaped by mechanization. Cars replaced horses. The telegraph revolutionized communications. Factories churned out goods at an unprecedented rate, driving down the cost to consumers.

Likewise, AI is revolutionizing how we live and work, how tasks are performed, and the speed at which things are created, and the next iteration of AI will likely have the ability not just to augment human capabilities but to replace them.

Is that a scary thought spelling the end of time and a robot takeover? Or is it a profoundly amazing opportunity for humans to step into roles that are more aligned with their natural gifts, challenging roles that liberate them from rote tasks and usher in opportunities for the highest level of expression?

AI isn't going anywhere. However, it's not AI that is upsetting the balance. It's society's unwillingness to adapt.

Leveraging the power of AI and embracing its capabilities can actually expedite equilibrium, as it can help us optimize processes, enhancing decision-making with unprecedented data analysis, and facilitate greater efficiency, which ultimately leads to higher profits.

In any business negotiation, it's imperative that we stay open to all disruptions.

Amit Kalantri wrote that the "telephone did not come into existence from the persistent improvement of the postcard."

The telephone, like all disruptive inventions, was born from a willingness to completely let go of what was true at that moment and conceptualize something even greater.

I have seen negotiations plunge south because of a stubborn refusal to adapt or improve upon conditions and expectations.

It's a rookie mistake to believe that victory lies in refusing to yield.

Flexibility is the mark of a pro.

The reality is that no one ever achieved anything ground-breaking by accepting the status quo.

MENTAL MASTERY AND ENDLESS POSSIBILITIES

Every moment of our lives we have to decide.

Do we see limits, or do we see possibilities?

My entire life I have challenged myself to push my own limits, and often it was because someone else told me I couldn't do it.

From an early age I learned to flip *no* to *on*. Tell me no, and my mind immediately responds with, "It's *on!*"

Not long ago I decided I wanted to be on national TV every week. Now I am. In college I was passionate about football and photography. I told a friend I had a dream of filming an NFL game. That declaration was met with a healthy dose of skepticism, which turned to shock when I called to tell him that I had just nailed a gig to become the photographer for the Arizona Cardinals.

When I decided I wanted a motorcycle, within six months I was riding on a professional circuit.

And swimming in a pool? Forget it. Throw me into frigid-cold waters off the coast of Maine, and let me battle hypothermia and panic attacks.

To be clear, I did not find that particular experience enjoyable, but I sure was proud to overcome it and make it to the finish line.

At one point I punched myself in the face to restore my vigor. If I was going to die in that water, I was going to die trying!

It was an exercise in assimilation, which I have found is a skill set that is vital to successful persuasion and negotiation.

Philosophically, our ability to win at anything, be it an Ironman or a contract negotiation, comes down to our mind's relationship to the environment we're in.

It's all an ecosystem that must be kept in balance.

In nature's ecosystem, if it gets too hot, too cold, or too polluted, or the environment changes too quickly, the system is thrown out of balance.

We've got to understand what each part of the ecosystem needs, how we fit into it, and when and what we need to adjust to cultivate harmony.

In any relationship, business or otherwise, success stems from all parties feeling that they have received equal value, perhaps not in percentages but in perception.

And the best leaders will work to achieve and restore this perception as often as needed, for as long as it takes.

Whether you're battling the unforgiving waves of the ocean or navigating the turbulent waters of deadlines and business negotiations, balance is not a destination but a constant endeavor, where empathy, flexibility, and the ongoing pursuit of value forge the path to mutual success.

About Mark

Mark Scribner, a managing director, partner, and wealth adviser at Carson Wealth, is a standout figure in the financial services sector, boasting over three decades of experience. Throughout his career he has shown a dedication to assisting clients in growing and safeguarding their wealth, guiding them through different life phases with skill and commitment.

Mark's enthusiasm for wealth management shines in his interactions with some of the families, individuals, and businesses across the United States. He excels at helping entrepreneurs achieve exits, ensuring that these crucial moments in their journey are handled with precision and compassion.

His expertise and wisdom are highly regarded not only by his clients but by major media outlets. Mark has been featured on NBC, CBS, Fox Business, PIX 11, and Newsy, and in esteemed publications such as the *Wall Street Journal*, the *Boston Globe*, and the *Washington Post*. This widespread recognition underscores his proficiency and impact in the realm of wealth management.

A proponent of learning and mentorship opportunities, Mark's commitment extends beyond his pursuits. He actively supports cancer research through fundraising initiatives aimed at combating this disease.

Mark's generous nature aligns with his hobbies, such as swimming and capturing NFL moments through photography. This unique combination reflects his personality.

For individuals looking for guidance in attaining wealth and navigating the intricacies of planning, connecting with Mark could be a transformative decision. His dedication to his clients and profession positions him as a resource in the journey toward stability and success.

In essence, Mark Scribner from Carson Wealth epitomizes wealth management. His wealth of experience, industry recognition, and unwavering commitment to both clients and charitable endeavors establish him as a figure in the realm of advisory.

#CarsonWealth #FinancialAdvisor #WealthManagement #TrueWealth

CHAPTER 4

THE FIVE PRINCIPLES OF IMPACTFUL LEADERSHIP

By Homer Smith

"A smooth sea never made a skilled sailor."
—FDR

Some people flee from complexity. Some run toward it.

My entire life I've felt called to helping people navigate their most important, complex, and difficult transitions.

In fact, it was an unprecedented and life-shaking event that took place in our country at the very beginning of my career that called me to do the work I do today.

It was September of 2001, and I had just graduated from college and started my career with a large national wealth-management company.

I was excited. I had studied hard, had passed all my licensing exams, and was ready to start building the career I had dreamed of.

I flipped on the news as I was getting ready for work when an image on the TV caught my attention. A small plane had crashed into one of the twin towers in NYC. By the time I had eaten breakfast and gathered my things to head to the office, the second plane had hit.

That was when the world finally understood that none of it was an accident.

I made my way to the office, still not fully grasping the magnitude of what was in progress. I walked in to find my colleagues gathered around the TV in silence. Together we watched as the towers fell, all aware that we were seeing history being altered and that life was about to look very different.

What happened next is somewhat of a blur. The market closed. No one was interested in talking about their retirement planning. As the news echoed our concerns about the resilience of the market, I began to question whether I had made the right career choice. I had worked so hard to get exactly where I was, only to have it come to a screeching halt.

What I realized is that in that moment clients didn't need an adviser to give them advice. They needed a leader to help them navigate this uncharted territory. It occurred to me that I could make the biggest impact in the world and on my clients' lives for generations by helping them navigate and plan for life's most difficult curveballs and transitions.

While many other financial advisers struggled to adapt to what was happening, I thrived and have since helped hundreds of clients through changes in their businesses, their personal lives, and the world.

I've come to realize that much of this success is derived from five simple principles of leadership. I have worked with everything from young families just beginning to build their wealth, to businesses and families worth hundreds of millions of dollars, and these principles apply to all of them.

They work well. They work fast. And best of all, they can apply to any industry, any market, any negotiation room, and any situation that requires tough transition.

QUIET THE NOISE

Have you ever been excited about a plan to spend the day outside, which got canceled because the weather app predicted rain, leaving you frustrated when the rain never came?

I'm guilty of that! Most people are. We allow external noise and predictions to steer us from our planned course. After 9/11 many of my colleagues stepped into the fear with their clients, and while their advice was well intended, it wasn't helping.

I survived because I discovered one of my superpowers. I could help my clients turn down the external noise, which was unpredictable and couldn't be proved, and focus instead on their goals and desires.

Six years later I moved to Hawaii to lead a team of twenty-five advisers just in time for what became the worst financial crisis since the Great Depression. Had I not gone through 9/11, I would not have been as confident in my ability to lead others through that transition.

There is an epidemic in many industries in which the experts, who in this case were financial advisers, make the mistake of selling themselves. They sit down with a prospective client and talk about the products they offer. They talk about their years of experience. They take up valuable minutes tooting their own horn instead of helping the client connect more deeply to their own goals and dreams. What I knew was that quieting the noise, focusing on the outcomes the clients want, and affirming their words back to them were the keys to surviving any temporary industry crisis.

Furthermore, I encouraged my team to lead prospective clients out of limited thinking. Often when people come to us, they're focused on what they don't have and what's not working. It's our job to lead them out of that limited thinking and paint a picture of what is possible and what could be true.

It worked. We became the number one–ranked branch office in our company.

It's not rocket science. We simply learned that we could persuade people to work with us by making sure the conversation wasn't about us at all.

SIMPLIFY COMPLEX CONCEPTS

Picture this: Your car is making a terrible noise and struggling to move, and you've got somewhere to be. You sputter into an auto center, and at that moment, you're not looking for a master class on the inner workings of engines. You just want the mechanic to wave their magic wrench and get you back on the road, pronto.

In my company we work with clients whose net worth is north of fifty million dollars. One might assume that anyone at that level is surrounded by world-class advisers who understand exactly what they need. What I have repeatedly found, however, is that many advisers are technically brilliant but lack an understanding of human behavior. They pepper their advice with complex words, complicated acronyms, and industry jargon to demonstrate their expertise, and end up frustrating the very people they want to impress.

I don't focus on what all the codes and accounts are called, but rather on what they can do for you. No one cares how the sausage is made; they just want to see results.

Anytime you're in a situation where you hope to establish trust and make an impact, work on simplifying the complex. Rather than getting caught up in showing how well you understand a concept or an industry, explain the advantages, the disadvantages, and how the other party can get exactly what they want. Most of the time people stay stuck in indecision because they're confused. If you can simplify the concept, you'll move the needle much faster.

A while back I was introduced to a family that owned a fourth-generation business and was deciding whether to sell. I was brought in because my area of expertise is helping businesses navigate complex transitions.

It was a highly stressful and emotional situation. After spending a considerable amount of time learning about the family's goals, I drafted a proposal, and the fee was significant. Their current advisers were a team in a big firm that had offered to handle the process for free with the implication that when they sold the business, their current team would manage the proceeds from the sale.

I explained to them that their current team would likely hand them a sixty-page brochure that outlined all the conflicts of interest and how the company would make their money back in return for offering this free service.

I wanted to manage their money too, of course, but I told them I would only expect them to work with me if I delivered the results they wanted.

I knew from our discussion that I could simplify the transaction process by having an investment banker on board who knew their industry well. I was able to line up discussions with two different bankers who gave them insight on what was happening in their industry as well as transaction trends to give them confidence in our process.

In the end they chose us because they wanted an objective view and because I simplified the process by focusing on the outcomes they wanted—a quick sale that still gave them fair value for their business.

Once the work began, I attended close to one hundred meetings between calls with the transaction team and with the clients to debrief them afterward and translate what was said.

It's important to remember that persuasion isn't about demonstrating authority and knowledge. As soon as the other party is intimidated or frustrated, you've constructed a wall that's tough to get around. Discover what's important to them, and explain in simple terms how your proposal helps them get it!

THE "EVERYONE WINS" PROCESS

I recently coauthored a book called *Making Smart Decisions: How Ultra-Wealthy Families Get Superior Wealth Planning Results.*

In that book my coauthors and I share a process that has proved to be hugely successful for all of us in our business interactions.

It's The 4-Step Everyone Wins Formula. You can use this

methodology in business and in life to massively increase your chances of a successful outcome. Here's how it works:

Step 1: Identify your self-interests.

Start by clarifying what winning means to you. Armed with that clarity, you can determine what you're looking for from your business relationships. This enables you to identify better areas of direct alignment or ways to deliver added value.

Step 2: Understand *their* self-interests.

The cornerstone to success is identifying what other people want. Become adept at unearthing what is positively meaningful (e.g., aspirations) and negatively consequential (e.g., fears).

Step 3: Appeal to their self-interests.

With a deep understanding of other people's interests, you can take two basic approaches: direct alignment and added value. With direct alignment, you concentrate on the overlap between your interests and those of the other party. The more overlap that exists, the easier it is to reach an agreement. By delivering added value, you use your capabilities, insights, and connections to help others achieve goals that differ from yours. When you help them achieve their objectives per the law of reciprocity, they are inclined to help you achieve yours.

Step 4: Track results.

As you use the "everyone wins" process, you only know if your actions have helped others achieve their objectives if you track results.

The "everyone wins" process is not the same as what most people would call a win-win outcome. In a win-win you are keeping score as if there is a finite pot to split. In the "everyone wins" process, you are aligning your interests and focusing on adding as much value as possible with the knowledge that this will likely result in a good outcome for you as well. The tracking component is not about keeping score of how much you win versus how much *they* win. It's about tracking how much of a positive impact you're making on the people you're working with.

By focusing on leading and helping others, you win. You win now and possibly in the future. You win in ways you weren't even thinking about because in your effort to understand and help the other side, your perspective will be broadened, and the opportunities are expanded.

FAIR DOESN'T ALWAYS MEAN RIGHT

"But that's not fair!"

That's a phrase usually yelled by someone who feels they got the short end of a deal.

If you're a parent, you've heard it a million times!

The notion of fairness often lies at the center of every negotiation. However, fairness doesn't always align with what's morally or ethically right.

We work with a lot of families who own businesses and have multiple children. Typically, there are some children who work in the business and others who don't. In that case is it fair that a child who has taken zero interest in the business receives an equal cut of it?

The reality is that equal distribution often ends in conflict, and the business ends up in shambles.

During my time in corporate management, an adviser on my team was dramatically outperforming everyone else, so I hired an assistant for her. Immediately many of the other advisers started grumbling that it wasn't fair. However, fair does not always mean *equal*.

Her performance earned her the extra support.

The perception was that it was unfair, yet the other team members couldn't present any evidence as to why it was unfair.

In any negotiation the ability to navigate perceptions of fairness requires a delicate balance of empathy, logic, and persuasive communication.

MIRROR MORE THAN WORDS

One of the most effective tools in negotiation is the use of mirroring, which is repeating what the other party says and mirroring their body movements. I found, however, that mirroring *values* is an equally powerful strategy.

When I moved to Hawaii, I was warned by many people that the local Hawaiians weren't always accepting of people from the mainland, which made sense, given the history of the islands. As soon as my wife and I arrived, we fell in love with the laid-back culture and traditions of the Hawaiian people. I ditched my suit for the traditional aloha shirt, and we did our best to adopt their way of living.

I was immediately embraced by the community.

My colleagues who refused to assimilate had a harder time fitting in and often did not get the results they were looking for. What I had learned, and genuinely embraced, was that the Hawaiian people were not transactional. They wanted to share their culture and beliefs. They wanted to feel that I respected their rich heritage and understood their values.

I learned so much from my community and along the way built a very successful business.

We're back on the mainland now, but I've never forgotten the lesson that being genuinely curious about other people builds bridges that can lead to success.

And I still don't wear ties!

A MOUNTAIN WITH NO TOP

Have you ever felt as if life is just an endless range of mountains to climb? Have you set a financial goal that you thought would be the answer to all your problems, only to find out that it wasn't enough?

If so, you're right!

The key is to climb as though the mountains have no top. It

doesn't mean that you never succeed, but rather that the possibilities for where you'll land are endless.

As you climb higher and higher, the air becomes cleaner, the view becomes clearer, and your mind and body will become increasingly stronger.

I believe we are born only with possibility, but as we get older, the world likes to throw limitations and complications our way. However, we don't have to let life's curveballs knock us off the mountain.

What I've learned is that all of us have a reservoir of untapped potential, and if you just commit to your highest goals, simplify your path by focusing on what matters, and strive to create situations in which everyone wins, you'll see a much bigger vision of what's possible and become excited for a life and business that have no peaks, only endless possibilities.

About Homer

A Private Wealth Advisor with over twenty years of industry experience, Homer S. Smith IV, CFP®, CRPC®, CEBC™, has dedicated his practice to working with business owners and families of wealth with complex financial planning needs. His mission is to simplify the lives of his clients by quieting the noise that surrounds them both personally and in their business and allow them to focus on what matters most—their purpose and goals.

Homer has taken the best practices from across the industry and provides a family office framework that is tailored with your needs in mind. Homer develops and implements customized strategies and solutions delivering exceptional value to you and your loved ones.

Homer coauthored *Optimizing the Financial Lives of Clients*, a road map for working with CPAs to bring more value to their top clients through an elite wealth management approach.

He recently released a second book, *Making Smart Decisions: How Ultra-Wealthy Families Get Superior Wealth Planning Results*.

What Homer is known for more than anything else is helping successful families and business owners navigate life's most complex, difficult, and important transitions. This might be transitioning from owner-operator to just owner, or transitioning the business to the next generation or to an outside buyer, or transitioning their wealth to their heirs and causes they care about in a way that is positive and impactful.

At Konvergent Wealth Partners, Homer provides impactful solutions, learning what matters most to his clients, including their goals and aspirations as well as their concerns. Ultimately, he wants to know everything and everyone important to you and everything and everyone that will be impacted by your financial decisions. This allows Homer to know what strategies and solutions will bring the most value to you and your family.

Homer provides state-of-the-art strategies and solutions with the collaboration of his elite team of professionals. Aside from the Konvergent team, he has established a network of leading authorities nationally to help deliver for you when the time is right.

Homer is a graduate of Western Washington University with a bachelor of arts degree in finance and a minor in economics. He enjoys spending time with his wife and daughters—hiking, traveling, shuttling to and from activities, and playing outside on their property with their dogs as much as possible.

Office: 253-236-7000 | www.konvergentwealth.com
3312 Rosedale St. NW, #102, Gig Harbor, WA 98335

Investment advice offered through Integrated Financial Partners, doing business as Konvergent Wealth Partners, a registered investment adviser.

CHAPTER 5

FROM SHADOWS TO SPOTLIGHT

*The Power of Empathetical Influence
in Reshaping Lives*

By Radim Pařík

When she entered the room, I had no idea what was coming. I knew who she was. I had read her file.

Hana. Sixteen. Troubled. Defiant. Known for aggression.

She said nothing as she walked in and sat across from me. I waited for her to speak and tell me why she was there, but she remained silent, her eyes cast downward. On the outside she seemed like an impenetrable wall, but I saw a scared child underneath.

I said nothing. I could feel the turbulent storm swirling inside her, and I knew she needed to feel that she was in control of our interaction. I did my best to hold an energy of safety and acceptance for her.

The minutes stretched into hours.

I knew her silence was an active silence. She was deciding if she could trust me and mustering up the courage to speak.

When she finally did start to talk, her voice barely above a whisper, the story was absolutely devastating. Every word was infused with suffering.

She had been misused by her father from the time she was a very little girl. When she reached ten years of age and began to protest, he drugged her to keep her compliant.

He shared her with his friends.

He kept her in a tiny room for a week at a time with no food.

Each piece of the story she shared painted a vivid and appalling portrait of the very worst examples of human depravity.

When I was sure she was finished, I spoke carefully. "It seems that no one would survive the journey you have been on." She lifted her eyes and said, "I feel like you are the first one who understands. I was thinking every day about suicide."

Hana came to me through my work with an organization called Summer Entrepreneurship Camp. Our mission was to organize business camps for children and youth from children's homes, asylums, and socially disadvantaged families.

I spent time there every summer teaching the children how to solve conflicts without fighting, how to listen actively to find common ground and interests, how to de-escalate conflicts, and how to negotiate.

Needless to say, it was a challenging environment, as most of the kids who came to us had experienced the very worst in life.

But her case was particularly traumatic.

We talked for several more hours about negative emotions, frustration and anger and the feeling of being totally alone.

By the end of our time together I could see that something had shifted. There is a very real physical transformation that occurs when someone feels heard. Their eyes meet yours. Their shoulders drop the tension they've been holding for years. Their posture relaxes.

I pointed out to her that while unspeakable things had happened, she had *survived*.

She was alive to choose her own future.

I am happy to say that today she is thriving! She has a very popular podcast in the Czech Republic and is telling her stories. They are the stories of thousands of children, and her work inspires others to heal. In the very first episode of her podcast she said, "Thank you," to me.

Sometimes the greatest and most important negotiations you'll ever lead have nothing to do with contracts, dollars, and cents. Sometimes it is about persuading other people to bet on themselves, to heal and to choose a new story of their own making.

Today I am an international strategic negotiator, a best-selling author, and the president of The Association of Negotiators. I've had the privilege of traveling all over the world to train with FBI agents and other professionals in the art of negotiations.

Yet my greatest work, and that of which I am most proud, is using the skills I have cultivated in my career to help those children reshape their lives.

How to Negotiate *Anything*

Negotiation is at play nearly every day for every one of us.

We consistently engage in the art of negotiation whether we realize it or not.

From the heated contract negotiation in the boardroom, to the agreements we come to with loved ones, to the price we are haggling over with the shop merchant, persuasive communication is happening all the time.

Most people, however, are doing it without strategy or guidance. Anyone can pick up a guitar and make noise with it. But only those who hire a teacher, take a course, and practice a set of steps are going to produce beautiful music!

The same is true for persuasive communication.

There are steps and tactics that if practiced will arm you with the ability to influence anyone, in any situation.

While we can't possibly cover everything you need to know in a single chapter, I want to share with you five strategies that when deployed will help you gain the upper hand in any situation so that you can lead all parties involved to the best possible outcome.

1. Create a Secure Base

Building a secure base in negotiation is like constructing any building or home.

It requires a solid foundation and reliable structure. Without that it could crumble at the slightest breeze.

When you are using persuasive communication, the structure of trust anchors the conversation and breaks down the walls between you and the other party. They no longer feel judged.

After all, you must build a bridge before you can cross it!

When you work to establish a secure base, you create an environment in which both parties feel safe to share their needs and stories. Once you establish emotional security, you are more likely to get the truth from them.

To do this, you've got to tap into your humanity. It's never just about the money. Let's say you are a real estate agent helping clients find a new home. They already have a home somewhere, so this isn't about putting a roof over them. There is something emotional behind their decision to buy a *new* home.

Maybe they feel the need to prove they are successful. Maybe they are moving to erase bad memories. Whatever the true reason is, it's your job to find it, name it, and persuade them that your option will help them get it.

Many times people will lie. They don't lie because they are bad people. They lie because they want to feel safe. They lie to save face. Sometimes they lie because they don't trust you and are afraid of your reaction.

That's why one of the trainings I offer is how to have X-ray vision and spot when someone is lying! Nonverbal communication is the strongest indicator of a lie in motion. If you watch closely, the other person's body will send signals before they speak. The limbic system is known as the "fast brain." If you stay alert, you will spot their physical cues. If someone leans back, it means something. That's your opportunity to say, "It seems like something crossed your mind just now."

To them it will feel as if you have read their mind. That is a powerful method for establishing trust and creating a secure base.

2. Focus on Emotions

One of the biggest mistakes I see negotiators make is that they focus on the transaction. They talk about money and contracts and fail to tune in to the emotions that are driving the entire conversation.

Life, fear, happiness, self-worth—these are the emotions that motivate people to make decisions. These are the emotional goals that cause us to enter a negotiation in the first place.

About a year ago a man came to me who was in a dispute with his partner over a construction project. It was a huge project, but a deep, personal conflict had brought the entire operation to a screeching halt. The partner hadn't paid my client in ten months, which meant my client now had no cash flow.

By the time he reached out to me for help, he was seething with a need for revenge.

He wanted to punish his partner. He wasn't interested in working out a new deal, or even working to save the project and company.

His entire focus was on destroying his business partner, who he felt had massively disrespected him. He was willing to spend the last of his money dragging his partner through court, his only goal being to destroy his partner's company and see him penniless.

I listened and validated his feelings. But then I asked him, "You have three hundred employees to think about too. Would you like them to see you as a leader who stands up and leads them to a new future? Or do you want them to see you as a hostage of this situation, a vindictive tyrant willing to burn it all down for the sake of revenge? How would you like your children and wife to remember you and your company?"

As I continued to talk about his family and the impact this war would have on their perception of him, I could see him begin to soften. The stubborn resolve he came in with began to dissipate, and I could see a shift in demeanor.

After a lengthy conversation driven by emotions, we were able to reframe his goal and, in doing so, reframed the legacy he would leave for his family and for the hundreds of employees who counted on him.

He came in as a bitter fighter. He walked out a hero.

3. Make *Everyone* a Hero

Everyone you encounter is engaging with life through a specific lens. They are hardwired with programming formed by their childhood, the way they've been treated, the experiences they've had, both good and bad, the traumas they've had to overcome.

The very nature of negotiations pits one side against the other, but that's a breeding ground for resentment and separation.

Trust is essential. Displaying empathy and being willing to step into the shoes of the other person help you shift from seeing them as the opposition to seeing them as the hero of their own story.

Remember Hana?

Many adults had already labeled her a lost cause. They were identifying her too strongly with her history, seeing only her file and not the person behind the story.

In my eyes Hana is a hero. Imagine living through such a nightmare and coming out of it alive, with your humanity and faith still intact. That takes heroism.

If you can do this and do it genuinely, you will find yourself easily establishing common ground with the other person.

Rather than seeing them as an adversary sent to disagree with you, see them as a hero, navigating their own epic story, fighting battles, and doing their best with the resources they were given to forge a good outcome for themselves and their loved ones.

When you do that, you unlock a higher level of empathy and are inspired to collaborate, rather than to just win.

4. Never Offer a Solution

In high-stakes negotiation, it is likely that the other party wants to feel that they are in control. That is why it's vital that you don't offer what sounds like a final solution.

Instead, offer two alternatives. Be sure that the first alternative you offer is an undesirable one and one you would never want them to accept. The second alternative should be the strong one that you hope they will agree to. Then let them choose.

What you've done is present them with a binary choice in which one option is obviously worse, yet by letting them choose, you've helped them maintain a feeling of autonomy.

This is not about finding alternatives that create a win-win. There is no such thing as a win-win. The famous negotiator Professor Blum says that compromise is the worst possible alternative you can accept. Everyone is a little bit unhappy with it. Sounds like a lose-lose to me! Win-win is ideology. Negotiating with a win-win outcome could theoretically work if the two of us had the same standard for what is fair. How do we measure what a win-win is? You can't.

We don't want to divide the pie into smaller pieces; we want to expand it so that everyone gets more.

Remember the construction guy who wanted revenge on his partner?

It turns out that the partner wasn't paying because they had not been able to secure loans from the bank. So it wasn't a matter of disrespect after all. It was a paperwork problem!

In the alternatives we presented, the partner could be dragged through court and spend hundreds of thousands of dollars they obviously didn't have, or they could allow us to speak to the bank on their behalf and negotiate a loan.

In the end that's what happened. We were able to secure them a loan that allowed them to pay what was owed and finish the project on time.

No one had to compromise or extend a deadline or go longer without cash flow. That's an example of baking a bigger pie!

5. Keep Your Bridges Intact

Finally, it's important to recognize that sometimes we reach an impasse, and a deal cannot be closed. That's OK.

I never burn bridges.

Stay kind, empathetic, and professional. The person who today is an opponent might want to hire you in the future. You never know when your paths will cross again. You never know when someone might come back with a changed mind and agree to your original deal.

Make the last impression they have of you a good one.

PERSUADE AND INSPIRE

I believe that if you have the skills to influence and solve conflict, you have a responsibility to use them. So many lives are upended by wars that never had to be fought.

Businesses are destroyed. Families are dragged through court systems. Countries go to battle. Destinies are missed. All because the first instinct was to fight rather than to negotiate.

If you commit to understanding how humans think and get intimate with the ways we learn to engage with life, you can become a powerful force for change.

Every child who comes through our camp has been fighting their whole life. They have fought for love, for food, for safety. They have fought to be heard and seen and validated. That's why I feel it is my moral imperative to foster an environment in which they can set down their armor and trust that I am not there to fight but to guide and inspire.

And I remember that when I am negotiating with adults too. Everyone has fought private battles of their own and is coming to the negotiating table with long-held points of view, old biases, and private dreams.

Embracing the responsibility to negotiate with empathy, curiosity, and compassion is not just a transactional decision but a calling—a chance to guide people to a better place, to reframe their perceptions of themselves, and ultimately to make the world a better, gentler place.

About Radim

Radim Pařík is an international professional negotiator, lecturer, leader, and sign language interpreter. He serves as the president of the Association of Negotiators and is a prolific speaker and author featured prominently in the Czech media landscape. Widely cited across television, radio, and newspapers, Radim stands as the most cited negotiator in the Czech Republic and Slovakia.

Radim is the acclaimed author of several books. Umění vyjednat cokoliv (*The Art of Negotiating Anything*) soared to best-seller status within five weeks of its release, and today it is the best-selling Czech book on negotiation. He is coauthor of the book *Empathetic Leadership* with the master negotiator, Chris Voss, which also hit Amazon's best-seller list this year.

Born in the Czech Republic, Radim's journey has led him across borders. He resided in Germany and subsequently in Poland. In both these nations he assumed prominent leadership roles within the multinational Schwarz Group, an enterprise that *Forbes* recognizes as one of the globe's top five–largest retailers.

After obtaining his MSc and MBA in strategic management from Nottingham Trent University, Radim earned his PhD in negotiation from LIGS University, where he realized extensive research on the most effective tactics used during negotiations. He further honed his negotiation skills through training under the guidance of multiple former FBI agents and completed the Harvard negotiation program, culminating in his graduation from the Harvard Negotiation Master Class. He is also a graduate of the Schranner Negotiation Institute and Advanced High Performance Leadership at IMD University led by George Kohlrieser.

Radim's educational achievements include graduating from the Certified Global Negotiator program at the University of St. Gallen and the Negotiation Program led by William Ury, as well as mastering negotiation techniques based on Mossad principles. He completed training in negotiating with kidnappers and terrorists from the international negotiation organization The Trusted Agency, the Hermione program.

He led the negotiation program at several European universities. Radim founded Fascinating Academy for commercial negotiation training, is the co-owner of PR PA RT NE RS Advisory Group, and initiated the

Association of Negotiators, uniting professionals across five countries on four continents.

He actively supports the blind and deaf people, is an ambassador for children from orphanages, helps them transition into their lives, and teaches them how to negotiate. Radim aids Top 100 Czech and Slovak companies for tough negotiations and lectures on negotiations for Security Information Service agents and top politicians. He earned the Czechoslovak LinkedIn Personality.

CONTACT RADIM AT:

Web: www.fascinating.academy
Email: fascinujte@fascinating.academy
Facebook: www.facebook.com/radim.parik
LinkedIn: www.linkedin.com/in/radim-parik
Instagram: www.instagram.com/radimparik

CHAPTER 6

UNYIELDING DETERMINATION

How Inner Power and Purpose Drive Massive Impact

By Patricia Santos

"I can't move my legs."

I tried again, suddenly unable to catch my breath.

"Why can't I move my legs?"

Around me the voices of the other agents seemed to blur, and all I could hear was the beating of my own heart and my inner voice willing my legs to move.

I had been in the meeting for hours, and now, as it concluded, I tried to stand up, but to my horror my legs wouldn't obey.

Panic set in, as it seemed that my brain could not direct my body into motion, and it didn't take long for the others to notice that something was terribly wrong.

Later at the hospital, an MRI revealed a serious issue on my vertebrae. The doctor walked into the room, and one look at his face told me that the prognosis wasn't good. If I wanted to walk normally, I would need major surgery, and there would be no more sport, no more exercise. "You will never run again," he said ominously.

As he rattled off a list of activities that I'd no longer be able to do, a spark was lit within me.

Suddenly logic didn't matter. The test results didn't matter. Even the fact that at that moment I couldn't stand up without falling over didn't matter.

No one was going to tell me that life as I knew it was over!

Inner Power Leads to Influence

In the quiet of February's chill, the journey began. I worked diligently to reinforce the muscles on my spine with the support of a personal trainer. Each session was a battle, not against the weights, or the resistance bands, but against the echo of a prognosis that sought to define limits where none should exist.

Pain became a familiar companion, a reminder of the struggle and the stakes. Yet with each passing day, the foundation grew stronger, my spine straighter, my steps surer.

The doctor's words hung in the air like a challenge, "You will never run again." They were not a deterrent but a spur, a reason to push harder, to prove not to the world but to myself that the human spirit is indomitable.

Even though I didn't like running, what I *really* didn't like was being told what I could and couldn't do!

August's sun bore witness to defiance. Vacation time, a period meant for rest, transformed into a crucible of determination. The first run—a mere one hundred meters—felt like an odyssey. Lungs burning, heart pounding, the finish line seemed an eternity away. But the goal was etched not in distance but in resolve. "Just a little better than yesterday" became my mantra.

As the month waned, so did the shadows of doubt. Eight kilometers of asphalt lay behind, a testament to willpower, to the refusal to accept the word *never*.

And in 2018, a year following the stark proclamation from my doctor, I crossed the finish line of the half-marathon.

There is power in the stubborn belief in your own abilities! Most of the limits placed on us are self-inflicted or put there by other people.

But we do have the power to ignore them and persevere.

When you prove to yourself that you can do anything you set your mind to, you cultivate a deep sense of confidence, which is a quality that is required for successful leadership.

When you step into a negotiation with confidence and

conviction, you carry yourself with an energy that naturally establishes trust and authority.

From that position you can capture the attention of your audience and guide the conversation in the direction it needs to go.

PURPOSE LEADS TO PERSUASION

I started my career as a health and safety coordinator, then a project manager on a wind farm, with no plan to enter the real estate market.

That all changed with a rubber chicken.

I had started to feel restless in my career. I'd been thinking of starting my own business but wasn't sure what I wanted to do. At that same time, my family had decided to move from Lisbon back to Braga.

Four years earlier I had worked with a wonderful real estate agent to sell my house in Braga, and every year for four years he would send me a postcard on my birthday and for Christmas. So when it was time to move back to Braga, I needed to buy a house and immediately thought of him.

We decided to meet for coffee, and when he walked in, he put a rubber chicken on the table.

At first, I thought he had lost his mind! But then he said, "Don't you remember, Patricia? This is your dog's rubber chicken toy. You accidentally left it in the house when you moved."

I couldn't believe it! He had held on to that toy for four years, waiting for an opportunity to give it back to me. I was so touched.

In that moment, I realized that real estate wasn't just about buying and selling homes. It was about personal connections and the impact we can make in each other's lives.

It was about empathy and humanity.

It was about noticing a problem and stepping in to fix it.

Throughout my entire life I've always been drawn to fixing problems. If I saw a potential for injustice, I had to act!

My mother often tells a story of when I was a little girl and accompanied her to the grocery store. Outside the store there were homeless children. It always hurt my heart to see them struggling. That day, my mother turned and noticed I was gone. She panicked.

A few minutes later the store manager found me outside, my arms loaded with candy from inside the store, handing it out to the children. My mother was so embarrassed and scared that we would have to pay for the candy, but the manager said, "No, it's OK. She is not stealing it. She is giving it to the hungry children."

It has always been my instinct to jump in and advocate for anyone who was struggling. If I see a problem that needs to be solved and I have a solution, I'm on it!

Now I express my purpose through my work, helping people, both clients and agents, to better their lives.

The care I felt from that agent made me realize that finding a home for one's family is a deeply emotional journey but one that is fraught with complicated paperwork and intimidating laws.

That's a problem. And solving problems is what I do best.

Today I am the cofounder and chairwomen of Zome, a leading benchmark in Portugal's real estate and agent training sector.

I love my work, and the company we built has impacted thousands of lives.

And for me it all started with a rubber chicken.

Respect Leads to Progress

Before I started my real estate firm, I was working as a health and safety coordinator. I was anxious to develop my career as a project manager but was having trouble finding a position that excited me.

That was when my phone broke.

My husband had two phones, so while I waited to replace mine, I was using his. One day a recruiter called looking for my husband, to offer him the job of project manager for a wind farm. My husband had previously applied for a quality manager position, and we had just started our own business, so he didn't want the job...but I did!

I made my pitch. The recruiter was familiar with my work and had heard that I was known for leading with ethics. I had a reputation for persuading people to do the right thing regardless of their position and for holding people accountable no matter what their title was.

He offered me the job. It would cut my salary by 50 percent, but I was ready for a challenge, so I accepted.

My first project was in total chaos when I arrived.

The project had been massively delayed, and my team now had just fifteen days to get a wind turbine assembled. I asked to go to the site and wasn't at all prepared for the mess I walked into! No part of the turbine was assembled, and it didn't take long to see why. The team was made up of experts from Portugal, Denmark, and India. Not only were there language and cultural barriers, but the Danish didn't get along with Indians, and no one on the team believed they could get the job done.

The client was very upset, as they had a contractual milestone to hit, and if the work wasn't finished on time, they would be penalized millions of euros.

I gathered the team. After a long inquiry in which I invited each group to share their desires and frustrations, we had a breakthrough. It was clear that each team was an expert in a certain part of the process. If I could get them to respect and celebrate their differences, they would see that diversity was not a hindrance but a massive benefit.

I told them there was no room for the word *impossible* and encouraged them to leverage one another's strengths and get the job done. My goal was to have each person only working in their area of expertise so we could work in a kind of assembly line rather than a chaotic mess.

They began to respect the fact that each of them was bringing a unique expertise, and every one of them chose to work overtime and to work together.

On the very last day at 11:00 p.m. the turbine was assembled. We hit our deadline.

Within a year and a half of taking that job, I became the director of all project managers and had more than doubled my salary from my previous job.

All it took was an ongoing commitment to seeing differences as an advantage rather than a barrier.

COURAGE LEADS TO CHANGE

Back when I was trying to mentor that team of engineers to construct the turbine, I was the only one who thought it was possible. I boldly declared that not meeting our deadline wasn't an option and that we would definitely be successful. These days, no one wants to promise anything!

If you want to be a strong leader and make an impact in people's lives, you have to have the courage to tolerate discomfort and to say what no one else is willing to say.

You must be willing to take extreme ownership, make bold claims, and have uncomfortable conversations.

Years ago one of my team members was struggling with a major drug problem.

I needed to have a conversation with him. I liked him, but I told him that I knew what was going on and that if he wanted to continue to work with us, he had to go to treatment. If he recovered, his job would be waiting for him. If he didn't recover, we'd have to part ways.

It was tough. He didn't want to admit the problem, and I found it difficult to confront him. Luckily, after a meaningful chat he agreed to treatment. Now he is clean, got married, and has a successful career!

CURIOSITY LEADS TO INNOVATION

"Mom, what are ethics?"

We were just finishing dinner when my twelve-year-old daughter asked me that question.

Instantly the answer comes out: "It's doing what's right!"

"How do I know what's right?"

It's tricky to explain to a twelve-year-old child concepts such as ethics, honor, and persistence, and the more I tried, the more questions she asked.

It occurred to me then that we can learn from a child's persistence in asking questions.

Children are endlessly curious. They want to learn. They're eager to soak up as much knowledge as they can.

What I have learned throughout my career is that great companies are made of great leaders, and great leaders ask great questions!

If you want to make an impact, on a team, in an industry, or in the world, you've got to get curious.

When we first started in the real estate business, I was shocked to find that there were no processes or procedures for how a transaction should be carried out. Everyone was working without standards. I knew my engineering background could help streamline the flow of selling a house and if I could systematize the process, more time could be spent on building quality relationships.

Years later when we started Zome, our own concept of a Real Estate Business Franchise, it was based in a neuroscientific study. We were living in a digital generation, yet the real estate market was still operating as though it were 1980!

The market was changing, the needs of the clients were changing, and the challenges faced by agents were changing. Everyone involved needed a model to follow. They needed scripts and routines and automation.

I was intently curious about how we could fix this problem.

My goal was to conduct a study that would ask questions about each stage of the transaction process and get a feel for the desires and challenges of everyone involved.

If we could find the intersection of commonality between agents, firms, and clients, we could build out a technology and a training program that would meet the needs of each.

The more questions we asked, the more insight we gained, and soon we were able to build out the most robust technology and software on the market to help agents be successful.

We developed the policies and procedures, the training programs, and the templates that would minimize paperwork and allow the agents more time to develop connections.

It worked, and today our company has the highest level of productivity in the Portuguese market and has earned multiple accolades, including the prestigious National WEB3 Innovation Award, recognition as the Best Company to Work For in the sector, and the 5-Star Award in the Franchising category.

Curiosity and empathy transformed an entire industry!

Passion Leads to Success

In 1642 Sir Thomas Browne wrote: "I am the happiest man alive. I have that in me that can convert poverty to riches, adversity to prosperity, and I am more invulnerable than Achilles; fortune hath not one place to hit me."

What kind of remarkable machine did this gentleman have in his head?

The same remarkable machine we all have. What Dan Gilbert calls a "psychological immune system." A system of cognitive processes that help us change our view so we can feel better about the world we are in.

Like Sir Thomas, we all have this machine. We've just got to use it!

I have created a very happy and successful life, and now my goal is to help others do the same.

If we can master the art of influencing ourselves, express our purpose in ways that are meaningful, and be genuinely interested in solving problems for other people, the possibilities for growth are endless.

And success is the natural result.

About Patricia

As a mother of two wonderful daughters, her greatest mission is to nurture those around her, guiding them toward their full potential. Her journey as a businesswoman, while fulfilling, is merely a vehicle to drive positive change in the world.

Her journey in the corporate world is marked by a relentless pursuit of innovation and excellence. With a degree in engineering and industrial management and specialized training in NLP, coaching, and neurocommunication, she has established herself as a leader in the business world. Her twenty-six-year tenure is distinguished by strategic roles in project management, business development, and leadership, collaborating with industry titans across the globe such as General Electric, EDP, Nortel Networks, Suzlon, and Vestas.

Her journey into real estate was driven by a strong desire to connect with people and help them develop their hidden talents. She used her skills in organizing and simplifying processes to build better relationships with clients. Currently, she is the cofounder and president of Zome Real Estate, and she served as CEO for the first five years and laid the foundation for the company's ascent, earning the company multiple accolades, including the prestigious National WEB3 Innovation Award, recognition as the Best Company to Work For in the sector and the 5-Star Award in the Franchising category.

While she cherishes the array of prestigious honors, she finds her true measure of success in the impact she imparts on people's lives—the enduring relationships she forges and the personal growth she inspires.

In addition to her business pursuits, she is a mentor and trainer specializing in leadership and talent management within the Voice Leadership program at the prestigious Nova School of Business and Economics.

Beyond her professional endeavors she is deeply passionate about issues such as sustainability and the transformative potential of blockchain technology. As the Portugal Country Chair of G100 Women Leaders in the Wing Leadership and Entrepreneurial Education, she undertakes a voluntary mission to champion inclusivity and the socioeconomic empowerment of women, actively addressing gender disparities.

Her mantra: "If you can't do everything, do everything you can. Don't settle for mediocrity; strive to be your best self! Embrace challenges, for they may unveil the greatest version of you yet to emerge. Take pride in proclaiming, 'It wasn't easy, but I achieved it!'"

For it's not only about succeeding in life but also about nurturing better human beings for the world.

Learn more at www.linkedin.com/in/patriciamentor.

CHAPTER 7

STRIKING ACCORD

The Art of Agreement

By Blair Lukan

"Where am I?"

As I gained consciousness, I could make out the faint scent of antiseptic and the buzz and beeps of medical equipment, but I could not remember how I ended up in that hospital bed.

"What happened?"

I was awake only a few seconds before the pain of broken bones set in.

"Why can't I move?"

Within a few minutes I was surrounded by doctors and learned that I'd been in an accident on my mountain bike.

My skull was broken, as was my left wrist, my right elbow, and my hip.

It was the summer before eighth grade, and even in my sleepy state I knew that life was about to be very different.

There would be months of physical rehab.

What I didn't know at the time was that this moment might mark the end of some things, but it marked the beginning of another—a transformative journey that would lead me to find my true calling in life.

After the accident I continued to struggle. I was physically limited and very self-conscious about the contraption on my arm that made me look like a robot.

What I *could* do was hang out with my friends. One day we

headed to the bookstore. It was a favorite hangout for us, and we always walked straight back to the sports section. As I followed behind my buddies, I happened to glance to my right. What I saw was a section called "Self-Help/Psychology." At that age, I didn't realize that people wrote books about how to get better at things.

I saw books with titles such as *How to Win Friends and Influence People* and *Your Infinite Power to Be Rich.*

I never made it to the sports section.

After that day, I became a voracious reader, devouring everything I could on how to improve my mindset.

It was a life-altering lesson on what I could and couldn't control and how to cultivate resilience in the face of what felt like impossible circumstances.

I couldn't ride. I couldn't run. But I could read. I could reshape my brain. I could train myself to form new neural pathways, and that's exactly what I did.

Later, much to the chagrin of doctors, I got back on the bike and returned to as many sports as I could. I had a newfound respect for the concept of helping oneself.

Persuasion Isn't a Tactic; It's a Duty

Today, I'm honored to advise hundreds of families on their wealth. My recommendations are framed in the same principles of resilience, negotiation, and communication that I've been reading about my whole life. I help people focus on what is in their control.

Before I recommend a financial strategy, I want to know the *why*. If you want to retire by sixty, I'll ask why. Questions help me uncover what really matters to you. My work isn't about money for money's sake; it's about what you want your money to do for you. Knowing your *why* lets me do my best work finding the investments that will deliver the life you envision.

In my life I strive for clarity and being present in the moment. In my work I see financial concerns keeping many people from enjoying the present moment. It's all about "staying tuned." I am a certified Peak Performance Coach with the Flow Research Collective, helping leaders and their teams reach their potential by having their biology work for them instead of against them.

My why is personal growth.

My purpose is to bring clarity and confidence to others through energy and attention management. But I realized that before I could coach anyone into changing their circumstances, I had to shift my perspective on persuasion.

Imagine someone you love needs a life-saving medicine. It's in their best interest to cooperate. Would you feel manipulative persuading them to take the medicine? Of course not! Your intentions are pure.

My belief is that if I have someone's best interest at heart, it is my *duty* to be as persuasive as I possibly can be.

THE LIGHT BULB MOMENT

When I was practicing to be a professional coach, I had a mentor who would review my coaching calls to build my skill set. I thought I was doing great, because in a thirty-minute call I was getting people to agree quickly on what they wanted to change.

I assumed my mentor would be happy. What I learned was that getting to agreement on what someone wants to work on, even if it takes most of the session, can be the most valuable part of the discussion.

When you're trying to help someone, being curious and reaching an understanding of what's most important to them is critical. My light bulb moment was realizing that if I listened well enough and asked questions, the client would often have a light bulb moment of their own.

I was learning to strike a chord, by striking accord. *Accord* is defined as (1) give or grant someone (power, status, or recognition), and (2) be harmonious or consistent with.

I am an avid music lover. When a chord is struck musically, it resonates with us and creates a memorable experience. The way to have our conversation resonate with others is through striking *accord*.

I read an article in which a man commented that science is distributed all over the world. However, technology is not. Most of the technological innovations are highly concentrated in certain areas of the world.

Technology is the *application* of science. You can have all the knowledge in the world, but knowledge is only potential power; what activates it is behavior.

Through my own journey of resilience, I became fascinated by the brain, not just how it works but the *application* of its capabilities. How do we apply what we know? What is the technology behind striking accord?

You see, the brain, contrary to popular belief, is not wired to store information but to recognize patterns. In those early coaching calls I was distracted by things in my mind, such as my to-do list. By storing things in my mind, I was diluting the brain's power of recognizing patterns in my clients' thinking. I learned to develop systems so that to-dos were stored outside my mind so I could be present with the other person.

As an example, have you ever tried to reason with someone when they're in a highly emotional state? You're trying to share logic, but in their heightened state the logical side of their brain shuts down. If you're not present, you won't notice, and your well-meaning advice will fall on deaf ears. How do we move someone from emotions to thinking logically?

I learned that the way was through listening, sitting with my clients while they rode waves of emotions and asking questions that helped them transition to logic on their own.

You can see the moment a person shifts from emotion to logic. Their posture rises, their face lifts, and confusion is replaced by a sense of empowerment.

The principles of Striking Accord are something I use every day in all areas of my life. I developed an acronym for the word *striking* that reminds me of the important components of a conversation and how to reach agreement.

S—Seek to understand.

Begin by positioning yourself in a mindset ready to fully grasp the other party's viewpoint by being present, and listening actively, seeking to understand, not to be understood.

One day my son came home, and I recognized that something was off. Anytime I notice my kids struggling with something, I invite them to take a drive. It's the perfect setup because it creates a safe space, free from distractions, without any uncomfortable eye contact. They always talk more when they don't have to look at me! As he shared what he was grappling with, I resisted the urge to go into "dad mode" and fix it.

Instead, I listened. When we got out of the car, he said, "Dad, I don't know how to thank you." The funny thing was, I hadn't said a word! I was just there, listening, letting him know he was being heard. He had come to the solution on his own!

T—Think empathetically.

The strongest rapport is built when we can put ourselves in the shoes of the other party to understand their emotions and underlying motivations.

Imagine you're constructing a bridge across a wide chasm. Before construction can begin, you've got to visit both sides of the chasm to see what kind of terrain you're dealing with.

The same is true in persuasive communication. You've got to do a survey of the emotional and psychological landscape of the other party before you can even begin to suggest a new perspective.

In construction the strongest bridges are built on a solid foundation. In interpersonal communications, the strongest bridges are built with empathy.

R—Reflect thoughtfully.

Take a moment to consider your responses carefully, stating back what you hear to confirm understanding.

Never be afraid of a pause. Comfortable silence is a powerful tool.

The person you're talking to will have a natural urge to fill the silence, and that's sometimes when they express the most profound things.

Formulate your next question after they are done talking, not during. You will find as you're thinking of your next question, they will fill that space with more information.

I—Illuminate priorities.

Sometimes what someone says they want is standing in front of what they *actually* want.

I see this a lot in my work. People say they want to be independently wealthy, but inquiring further, we find that the root is they want time and freedom to be with their family and take care of them.

Shine a light on what is most important to the party involved. Remind them of their core objectives to keep the focus of the conversation on what matters most.

K—Kindle flexibility.

Ignite a spirit of adaptability, encouraging all participants to remain open to new ideas and willing to adjust positions. Avoid jumping to conclusions and solutions.

Imagine the conversation you're having as a winding river.

The river's nature is to flow. Sometimes it flows smoothly and uninterrupted. Other times it hits against fallen trees and rocks. But the river doesn't stop in its tracks at the first sign of obstruction. It simply adjusts its path and goes around whatever is standing in its way. Water is patient, it can be forced to change its course, but it isn't frustrated. Water is unafraid to explore.

If you can practice this same flexibility during any communication, you can learn to navigate obstacles and objections and adjust your approach.

I—Investigate deeply.

In my first job out of school I was an account manager with a company, and the management team sent a group of us to hear a speaker who was an expert in sales.

I was in awe of the advice he shared.

After the session, he encouraged each of us to go back to

whatever account we were struggling to get and try his strategies. I was nervous. I called the speaker and told him I was about to approach an engineering firm that had been doing business with a competitor for over ten years. I told him I thought I needed to do research on engineering firms before proceeding.

He told me that the less I knew, the better because I wouldn't make any assumptions.

He encouraged me to ask a ton of questions and stay curious throughout the whole appointment with the goal of discovering how we could be of service.

By the end of that appointment, I got their business!

N—Nurture insights continually.

As a lifelong student of psychology, I found myself wanting to bring the principles of personal development to my team. The idea was to create a culture within a culture and foster a continual, enriching dialogue that would lead us all to deeper insights.

The more we practiced empathy with one another, the more we began to understand how to help each other be successful.

How many times have we passed judgment on the colleague who leaves early without bothering to find out why they do it?

How often have we assumed that someone is antisocial because they don't chat in the breakroom, rather than getting curious as to *why*?

The more we remained curious, the better we were able to come together as a team that learned to magnify strengths and leverage our differences.

G—Guide toward agreement.

One of the biggest mistakes leaders make is failing to lead conversations toward a consensus. They make assumptions about what's important and in their rush waste resources and solve the wrong problems.

Getting to agreement is critical. By repeating back what you have heard, you find out if you have understood, and if not, you dig more until you reach a consensus. It is the greatest way to identify the real issue and help others feel as if they have been understood.

If you can strike accord, and reach agreement on what to focus on, you can then move on to the *how* of achieving what is most important to the other person.

Leading with Empathy

Growing up, I heard a lot of stories about my grandpa Lukan. He moved from Minnesota to Canada to Homestead. I remember my father telling me that my grandpa never worked a day in his life for anyone else. Throughout his life he had had a hardware store, a livestock business, and a fuel delivery business, among others. He sounded like a hard worker, but it was the freedom that stood out to me, the freedom to live life as he chose to live it.

When he came to Canada, it was close to the turn of the last century. My father would tell me that during the height of the Great Depression my grandpa always had money in his pocket and was always willing to use it to help. If someone needed to sell something to feed their family, he was ready to do business and fairly. It's from those stories that I first encountered the importance of ethics in business.

Today, with every team member or client I encounter, I ask myself, "If this were my sister or if these were my parents, how would I treat them? What would I want for them?"

In most negotiations, we are naturally wired to view the other party as the opposition.

What if instead we rewired our brains to see them as partners whose hearts are in the right place and whose goals are as worthy and valid as our own?

Just as a chord in a song requires the blending of individual strings to create a harmonious sound, we can learn to interact with one another by harmonizing our perspectives, cultivating understanding, and ultimately, working together to strike accord and create!

About Blair

Recognized as a leading financial adviser and a principal at Edward Jones, Blair Lukan has helped hundreds of people achieve their financial security goals. Understanding his clients' *why* enables him to tailor investments and solutions to align with their highest aspirations. His unique and highly sought-after approach transcends mere monetary gain, focusing instead on realizing his clients' dreams through the vehicle of their financial endeavors.

Believing in the power of long-term planning, he advocates for crafting written financial strategies rooted in personal motivations. Blair expertly guides clients toward achieving their objectives over the span of a life-time, fostering a steadfast commitment to long-term financial success despite market fluctuations or emotional impulses.

Embracing clarity and presence in both his personal and professional life, he recognizes the role of financial concerns in hindering the enjoy-ment of the present moment. Drawing from practices such as medita-tion and yoga, he seeks to instill mindfulness in his approach to financial planning, empowering clients to navigate their financial journeys with intention and serenity.

Additionally, Blair is deeply engaged in the study of optimal human performance through his involvement with the Flow Research Collective, where he is a certified peak performance coach.

Outside of his professional endeavors, he finds solace and adventure at his family's lakeside cottage, and in activities such as fishing and snowmobiling.

To learn more or to contact Blair, visit the following:

- edwardjones.ca/blair-lukan
- linkedin.com/in/ejadvisorblairlukan
- facebook.com/ejadvisorblairlukan

CHAPTER 8

INFLUENCING—THERE AIN'T NO APP FOR THAT!

By Ed Piergies

I rounded the corner and was smacked in the face by the heat and taste of metal. I walked hesitantly through the smoke-filled factory, the hum and clank of machinery muffling the men's voices as my young eyes searched through the haze of sparks for the familiar face I was seeking. This daunting place that both fascinated and terrified me was called The American Crucible, and it was the factory my father worked at for forty years.

These were the earliest memories I had of my father. He was a first-generation Polish American, and like so many others of that generation, he struggled and hustled to feed his family. Dad was a pump assembler. It was a humble title with a humble paycheck accompanying it. But there was plenty of love. I can still picture his face, covered in sweat and grime but always beaming with a smile when he saw me walking through the factory carrying his lunch box.

My dad would give anyone the shirt off his back. If you could imagine combining Andy Griffith with Jimmy Stewart from *It's a Wonderful Life*, that was Dad. His factory was only ten minutes from the house, so every now and then one of us four kids would take him his lunch. When it was my turn, I was always teetering between the excitement of seeing Dad and the terror of being engulfed in this weird dystopia of metal and fire. I know now that it wasn't about lunch.

Exposing my siblings and me to the factory was all part of his plan. He wanted his sons to wear suits to work every day, to avoid the hard labor he was subjected to, and to never forget to look out for the little guy.

Years later I found myself as the hiring authority for a billion-dollar company, wearing a suit daily and covering twenty-eight states. Even though Dad was proud of me, I couldn't shake the feeling that I wasn't quite embodying his legacy of genuine kindness and consideration. You see, twenty-eight states is a lot of turf for one person to cover, so I hired recruiting firms out of sheer need.

The experience was terrible.

I called them headhunters (and a few other names unsuitable for print). Each promised to be a caring problem solver. But in the end they only sent gobs of no-fit resumes for me to comb through. So I was drowning in resumes but starving for talent...and wasting a lot of my time.

Not only could I not find any loyalty, but I struggled to find basic competence! They neglected to mention that their industry had up to a 90 percent turnover rate each year. This couldn't possibly be the path that my dad had in mind for me, and every day, I could feel my own discontent growing, my values in complete misalignment with those in this field.

The recruiting industry's disconnection and lack of trust became apparent from every angle. They were interested in volume over quality and fee collection over proper talent placement. It was incredibly frustrating and, more than once, made me question my faith in my fellow man! It was like *The Hunger Games*, everyone looking out for themselves, meeting quotas and more than happy to step on or disregard anyone who got in their way. I wasn't having it.

Is this really what it's about, completely ignoring the needs and aspirations of others to meet a few KPIs? Other than the spouse you select in life, where you work is one of the most life-affecting decisions you can make—shouldn't that be taken into consideration?

HAND ME MY CAPE

The industry needed a hero. And by hero, I mean someone who was vulnerable, listened, and cared whether people ended up happy! I felt a compelling need to transform the industry's transactional nature and build a company that focused on service, collaboration, and trust. It was time to open a game-changing, industry-disrupting recruiting firm—a recruiting firm with a conscience!

At first, I wasn't sure how I was going to do it. After all, anyone who had ever worked with a recruiter would come in bruised, skeptical, and poised to fight. Then I saw the movie *The Horse Whisperer*, and the dots instantly connected in my mind.

In it Tom Booker, a unique horse trainer, rebels against the old established ways of doing things, and typically, training a wild horse involved whips, dust, and a lot of pain until the horse submitted. Tom came in and instead connected to the horse, approached it on its terms and learned to speak its language. This painless, gentle, and collaborative approach worked leaps and bounds better than the abusive tactics of old.

That's when the light bulb went on. Most potential client firms have had rough experiences with recruiters before. It didn't take much to make them suspicious.

I would deploy this horse-whisperer energy into the recruiting industry, surprising everyone with a curveball of genuine interest, curiosity, and care.

Our mission for clients: Beyond recruiter, to become their secret weapon, partner, and brand ambassador.

Our mission for candidates: To not just change their business cards but change their lives.

During my initial months at the helm of CWP, I was tasked with a significant challenge: finding a chemical engineer for a company with a specific emphasis on diversity. I met with a wonderful couple of Asian descent. The wife was seeking a new position with a higher salary to support her husband's pursuit of a second PhD. This tiny, respectful couple won me over instantly. I had to help.

Determined to help, I asked her to share her desired income, and she specified $17,000. Against the odds, I secured a position for her offering a yearly salary of $68,000. When I delivered the news, her husband got up, walked around my desk, put his arms around me, and with his limited English said over and over, "Appreciate. Appreciate." At that moment, I felt like the hero I had hoped to be. I had found my calling.

CONNECTING THE DOTS: LIFE LESSONS FROM UNLIKELY PLACES

The dull glow of the overhead light threw shadows on the faces of the other poker players, obscuring their expressions and making it very difficult to guess their hands.

I was in a hand with Dr. Doug. Superman had Lex Luthor as his nemesis, and I had Dr. Doug at the poker table, always challenging me on the felt. I was impressed with the top pair I held until Dr. Doug raised three times what was already in the pot...and my top pair shriveled up like a spider on a hot stove. I folded. Laughing (evil laughter), Dr. Doug showed his bluff; he had nothing. Poker players go on what is called *tilt*, which means that out of anger, they blame everything imaginable for their loss—the cards, bad luck, the weather, Dr. Doug's dog...anything will do.

My wife and I are avid poker players, but we were facing a downturn in earnings. We decided to work with a poker coach, who imparted some crucial lessons.

"Ed," he said warmly, "you've got to hunt your own mistakes." He asked me why I lost that hand. I said it was because I was too conservative. He waited. I said it was because I relied too heavily on the math. He waited. Then he asked what Chris Voss would call a thought-shaping question: "How does your game appear to others?" I looked at the floor for several minutes, like a kid in the principal's office. I knew the answer. I didn't want to say it out loud. Finally, I said it. "Weak!" That moment of radical humility marked an upgrade in the evolution of how I handled fear in my game, my life, and my business. It's the breakthrough moment I try to get people to amid a career change. Life is like poker, a game of incomplete information. Sometimes you need to make a decision, back your judgment, and live with the results. It's all about how you marshal your resources under duress.

A critical ingredient to my firm's success is aligning ourselves with partner firms we genuinely believe in. On the candidate side, we mainly deal with high achievers who aren't seeking a new job. So there must be some *wow* factor, some reason for this to make sense for them. These high achievers we approach are working on great projects and are paid very well. So what's missing in their careers? Meaning, purpose, impact. In short, *character.*

Character-based people want character-based firms; they just can't find each other. That's where we come in.

Another critical ingredient for success is a high-character recruiting team. I do not hire recruiters. I hire "influencers and storytellers," and that has made all the difference in the world. The typical recruiting call can feel as if someone is trying to sell you a timeshare. With my team, people feel courted, not processed. Like the horse whisperer, there are no whips, dust, or pain involved with our process.

Character Precedes Successful Persuasion

I always joke that most recruiting agencies should have signs on the doors that say things like, "HERE, WE PRETEND TO CARE," and "DEPARTMENT OF REDUNDANCY DEPARTMENT."

Very few recruiting firms end up being helpful. They masquerade as a concerned guide, there to influence circumstances in favor of the candidate, but underneath the scripted pitch, they are just trying to make a sale.

Distinguishing selling from influencing mirrors the contrast between lust and love—while one seeks to *take from you*, the other aspires to *give to you*.

That's why it became my life mission to build a recruiting firm with a conscience that connects A+ people with A+ companies.

I aimed to create a company that redefined the industry narrative and shifted the focus from getting to giving.

Anytime you are committed to accomplishing a goal, it can be tempting to keep your eyes on *your* prize. What I've learned, however, is that the more people we help, the more we get what we want!

Giving precedes getting, and that value was born out of two remarkable influences in my life.

My father embodied the values of selflessness, humility, and unwavering commitment to family. His life was a testament to the importance of virtue over material success, teaching me that true happiness stems from kindness.

Contrasting with this gentle influence is my Greek best friend of fifty years, Kenny (Kyriakos), who embodied a cocktail blend of John Wayne toughness and James Bond cool. His charismatic persona presented a stark counterbalance to the softness of my father, but he never failed to display a depth of character beneath his rugged exterior. Through Kenny, I learned that coolness and goodness are not mutually exclusive. Kenny's nickname is El Cid, taken from the old movie starring Charlton Heston, where he was called El Cid because he had the power to make men greater than themselves. Legendary friend, legendary impact.

These two extremes have intricately shaped the person I am today. They underscore the overarching theme that character is paramount. I have learned that you are as successful as you are kind, but without courage, goodness is not possible—a reflection of the enduring impact these two influential figures had on the fabric of my character.

I have watched my competition lie, cut corners, throw their colleagues under the bus just to get ahead. I'm proud to say that my commitment to genuine kindness and connection has been very lucrative for our team.

Treating people with deference during negotiations is so rare these days that it becomes a competitive edge and a differentiator that not only makes you memorable but clinches you as the obvious choice. Out-listening and out-caring your competitors turns out to be a successful business strategy. Who knew?

Success Is All in Your Head . . . Literally

The greatest mistake in life is continually fearing that you will make one. As Cus D'Amato (Mike Tyson's trainer) said, "Fear is wetting your pants. Courage is moving forward with wet pants."

Nine times out of ten, when I meet with a client struggling to find their way in their professional life, the culprit isn't the market; it's their own mind!

You may remember that I had some adjustments to make to my poker game that involved taking responsibility for my own mistakes. That wasn't the only lesson I learned from that painful hand. My poker coach also taught me about the knowledge/action gap.

The knowledge/action gap happens when you know the correct move to make, but fear creeps in, overriding your knowledge and paralyzing you from taking any action at all.

Today, anyone with an internet connection has all they need to be rich and in shape. Yet few are. We all know we can get healthier by eating less and moving more. We know we can have more money by spending less and saving more. Yet for whatever reason, our minds talk us out of taking good-for-us actions.

I try to coach people going through the process of a career change to push through the knowledge/action gap, and that typically requires a lot of mindset coaching.

Usually, it starts with them holding tightly to a self-limiting belief, "This won't work."

It's up to me to shift that inner dialogue to an empowering

decision by encouraging them to ask themselves, "What would need to be true for this to work?" and then to ask them to come up with twelve reasons that this *would* work so they gather evidence for positive results.

Often they are focused on everything that could go wrong. A mindset coach taught me that your brain is like Google. Whatever we ask it for, it will run a search and deliver those specific results. Google "red jeeps," and you'll get a million pictures of red jeeps. Google "green jeeps," and you'll get a million pictures of green jeeps. Get the picture? The reasons to move forward are just as numerous as the reasons to take no action; we're just not searching for those.

And that's the two-millimeter shift that changes lives, that takes you from worry to positivity. By realigning your mindset, you can actually repurpose hours of fruitless worrying.

A positive outlook is far more than a mental preference. It changes your brain, literally. It's the nearest thing we have to magic. It's the key that unlocks the handcuffs of worry, self-doubt, and disbelief. Powerful, appropriate action from a negative state is difficult, if not impossible.

I'll leave you with this: Gravity, magnetism, electricity—forces of nature that are silent and invisible; we only notice them by their effects.

Influence is invisible too; we only notice it by its impact. Does your influence point others toward their true north?

About Ed

Ed was raised near Cleveland, Ohio, where he earned a BS in electrical engineering, a BA in business management, and an AS in general business, graduating with honors in all three. Education proved to be the pathway out of the rough neighborhood where he was raised, but as Ed says, "No one ever really goes to college to become a recruiter."

At age twenty-six, Ed designed and implemented a national recruiting program for a billion-dollar firm, where he trained fifteen divisions on hiring, strategy, and techniques. He managed technical recruiting efforts for a twenty-two-office recruiting firm, where he witnessed firsthand the broken and often combative nature of the recruiting industry. It was a high-turnover, volume-based industry where companies and candidates would utilize a recruiter only out of sheer desperation. Ed knew that if done correctly, recruiting could be impactful, life-changing work. A steady supply of superior talent gives any firm a sustained advantage over its competitors. But they must be deserving of such talent.

Imagine if companies posted ads for new clients the way they post ads for new employees—it would net them zero new clients. That's why no one does business development that way. You need to approach getting employees the same way you approach getting clients—you need to go out and get them! Overreliance on tech tools has made real recruiting/influencing a lost art. Influencing simply can't occur through a text or a one-minute, "drive-by" recruiting call.

So in 1993 Ed founded CWP Technical Group Inc., a recruiting firm that introduces character-based firms to character-driven people.

Over the years, with the help of many mentors/coaches, Ed perfected this character-based recruiting method. He has aligned his firm with a handful of rare, truly character-driven firms. "When you help build cultures you believe in, it doesn't even feel like work; it's more of a calling."

Upon reading *Never Split the Difference*, Ed was gobsmacked. Influencing people using deference and listening! Ever have that feeling on a Sunday where it seemed as if the preacher was speaking directly to you? Chris' techniques were the perfect bayonet to fit onto the end of the weapon Ed's company was already using...deference, compassion, and listening. Thanks, Chris!

CWP Technical Group specializes in construction, civil engineering design, architecture, the energy sector, and finance. CWP prides itself on being experts at becoming experts. They are also sought out for training, talent acquisition strategy, executive coaching, and speaking engagements.

Connect with Ed or CWP Technical Group:

- www.cwptechnical.com
- (937) 477-3808
- cwptech@cwptechnical.com
- www.linkedin.com/in/ed-piergies

P.S. In case you were wondering what CWP stands for, Ed named his company after his dad, Chester Walter Piergies.

CHAPTER 9

THE POWER OF PERSUASIVE STORYTELLING TO DRIVE CHANGE

By Nick Nanton

"It's just not a fit for us right now."

"Great idea, but not what we're looking for."

"It's a no for now."

I can't tell you how many times I've heard some version of that phrase, especially when I was first starting out.

It's a scene I've been in hundreds of times—the air thick with anticipation, the hum of uncertainty lingering between the phone lines, the awareness that the fate of my project hinged on my ability to inspire someone who barely knew me to listen, to feel something, and to jump on board.

You see, in addition to being a songwriter, an author, and a TV producer, I make documentary films.

And documentaries cost money to make. A lot of it!

Imagine trying to pitch your song or movie idea to industry giants who are bombarded with pitches all day long, and it's up to *you* to be different enough to get them to lean in and want to know more.

Luckily today, I've built enough of a solid reputation in the industry that I have a much easier time making these conversations happen, but still, it's a daunting task trying to get these big players to see the potential in my project as much as I do.

But my mission has always been to tell stories because I believe wholeheartedly that stories change lives.

I also believe that when a story goes *untold*, people who may have been helped by it are left vulnerable. So, it's pretty nerve-racking that the fate of every project rests almost entirely on my ability to enroll others in my vision.

There's always a make-or-break moment, a precipice between success and failure, during which I can feel the weight of every word I say shaping the destiny of the film.

This is where the art of persuasion comes into play!

I've discovered over the last twenty years that the art of persuasion isn't confined to the boardroom or the negotiating table. It's a skill that has colored every facet of my journey. From convincing stakeholders to believe in the uncharted territory of my ideas to rallying a team around a shared vision, persuasive communication has always been my ally.

And whether you realize it or not, it's yours too.

Odds are that nearly every day of your life, you encounter a situation that requires persuasion.

Whether you need to persuade a client to hire you or persuade a child to go to bed, how well you do it will determine if you end up celebrating a victory or nursing a disappointment!

Now, before I go further, I want to make sure I cover what persuasion is *not*.

It is not unethical.

It is not manipulative.

It does not begin and end with getting a signature on a dotted line, securing a deal, or closing a sale.

That kind of narrow interpretation overlooks the profound impact of persuasion on building connections, fostering trust, and nurturing lasting collaborations. The potency of persuasion extends far beyond the realm of the transactional.

You see, as an entrepreneur driven by the passion to make a difference, I came to realize that the true measure of success lies not just in the milestones achieved but in the enduring impact on the lives touched along the way.

And persuasion, when wielded with integrity and purpose, becomes a driving force behind the realization of shared goals. To limit its scope to a mere transaction is to overlook its potential to shape the very fabric of our human experience.

But how do you do it?

How do you use persuasion to achieve your goals without being self-serving? How do you leverage it to influence stakeholders and enact change?

I can tell you that after years of writing songs for the music industry, securing interviews with top celebrities, and making award-winning movies, I've distilled it down to a three-step formula. This formula, simple as it is, has allowed me to forge powerful partnerships with some of the world's most fascinating people, all while pursuing my own dream of telling stories that matter.

CHOOSE A CAUSE THAT'S BIGGER THAN YOURSELF

I want to make movies that change lives, movies that shine a giant spotlight on deeply moving stories, issues that need to be discussed and people who are changing the world with their purpose-driven work. It's both my mission and my passion.

None of the documentaries I make are about me. They aren't even about the people we film. They are about a bigger idea or cause that can shift the way others view their own lives or the way they approach an issue. When I take the idea to my potential partners and stakeholders, I am pretty confident they'll promote the cause. Very few people are going to say no to helping promote the cause of illiteracy or sex trafficking or bullying when it is presented in the right way.

But promoting a cause and financially supporting it are two very different things, so it's my job to shape the cause into a bigger picture that shows how their involvement will play a part in the improvement of humanity.

So, the first part of the persuasion formula is to zero in on a cause that's bigger than you.

Years ago I had the opportunity to meet the amazing Peter Diamandis.

Now, if you don't know who that is, he was named by *Fortune* as one of the World's 50 Greatest Leaders; he is the founder and executive chairman of the XPRIZE Foundation, which leads the world in designing and operating large-scale incentive competitions; he is a best-selling author; and he has started over twenty companies in the areas of longevity, space, venture capital, and education.

Early on he encountered skepticism and resistance from institutions that doubted the feasibility of his ambitious goals. Undeterred, Peter cofounded the XPRIZE Foundation, overcoming financial hurdles and skepticism to successfully incentivize private spaceflight.

When I approached him with my idea to make a movie about his story, he wasn't initially interested. He said something to the effect of, "Thanks, but I don't want a puff piece."

So, I said to him, "Peter, I'm not interested in a puff piece either. I am interested in a piece that shows the world who you are and how you do what you do so that all the other Peters who are sitting in their bedrooms or cubicles unfulfilled, stuck in the wrong line of work, and running out of time can reconnect to the dreams they put on hold. I want to inspire them by showing them that against all odds, they can achieve greatness and become the people they were born to be."

To which he replied something like, "Now *that* is a film I can get excited about."

At its core it wasn't a story about a man. It was bigger than that. It was about dreams, resilience, perseverance, and the vast storehouse of human potential.

Repeatedly, I have been able to persuade people to contribute their hard-earned dollars to causes that aren't always about getting a financial return because the cause was bigger than all of us and together we could create a ripple effect of impact much bigger than any of us could create on our own.

Together we've made films that have won many awards, have changed countless lives, and have even stopped a few suicides by showing hope to those who felt that nobody could understand their pain.

So, the next time you have to use persuasion, whether it's for a huge creative goal or to prove a point in a meeting, ask yourself this:

Is my mission here bigger than me?

Will it help the greater good?

Do I believe in this enough to put my fears and ego aside and ask for what I really want?

If you can answer yes to those questions, you're on the right track.

CREATE A WIN-WIN SCENARIO

When I decided I wanted to make documentaries, I never had any illusions that it was going to be easy. I knew that securing stakeholders was going to be a delicate dance. It wasn't just about presenting facts and figures; I had to illustrate how their participation could genuinely enhance *their* lives.

They needed to know that by investing in my movies, they were becoming a part of something bigger and accepting a special place in the arena of social change. That's why I created Abundance Studios—to cultivate a collective of entrepreneurs, professionals, and philanthropists who are dedicated to making media that inspires action, service, and change.

I never want to present people with a risky investment. That's what everyone else does! I want to extend an invitation to join an exclusive group of visionary minds that are *changing the world*. And no, it's not just a risky investment presented as an exclusive invitation; I engineered the entire opportunity of Abundance Studios to actually be something totally different, and that's how it keeps its integrity.

I want my Abundance Studios producers to know that by

supporting the causes I am bringing to them, they are investing in themselves and the chance to participate in amazing opportunities. In lieu of any risky financial ROI, I want them to see, just as I have, that personal growth and life experiences are a *guaranteed* investment.

That's the second part of the formula—make it a win for everyone involved.

But here's the golden rule: Stay authentic. Don't pretend to be something you're not. People appreciate honesty.

I go out of my way to make sure the Abundance Studios producers are given extraordinary, once-in-a-lifetime opportunities to be on movie sets, meet cultural icons, travel to incredible places, and sit at tables with people they can learn a lot from.

When people can see the direct and tangible benefits of supporting your cause, you're not just persuading them—you're inviting them into a mutually rewarding partnership with a broad and impactful reach.

TELL A GREAT STORY

The best tool in all our toolboxes is storytelling.

Storytelling is like the unsung hero of persuasion. It's not about bombarding people with numbers and jargon, but rather about sharing real-life narratives that win over hearts and minds.

All of us humans are living out a story. We are living the stories of our heritages, our relationships, our religions, our diagnoses, our healing journeys, and everything that makes us who we are. Early cave drawings showed us that stories were the very first language, and they continue to be a universal language we can all relate to.

Stories cut through the noise and connect us on a real, personal level. They are the difference between showing someone a spreadsheet and taking them on an adventure. Stories make your pitch memorable, relatable, and most importantly enjoyable.

That's because stories have the remarkable ability to transport your listeners beyond boardrooms and balance sheets and into a collective experience that resonates on a deeply personal level.

Through the artful crafting of stories, I have been able to paint vivid pictures that evoke empathy, ignite inspiration, and ultimately lead to a collective commitment toward a shared vision.

Often I do this by telling a story in which the facts are common sense but not common *knowledge*.

In 2020 I got an email from a guy named John Corcoran, who told me he was known as the teacher who couldn't read. Despite having already told his story on *The Oprah Winfrey Show* and *Larry King Live*, John felt that the issue of illiteracy needed an even bigger stage, and our mutual friend Jack Canfield (the cocreator of the wildly successful *Chicken Soup for the Soul* series) suggested he give me a call.

Now, common sense tells us that illiteracy is a problem. But what wasn't common *knowledge* is that in the United States, we have never passed a threshold of more than 40 percent of America being literate at the grade level they're supposed to be.

That means that 60 percent of Americans are not literate. They may not be illiterate, but they are *subliterate*, which means they can get by but aren't reading at a level that would test as fully literate.

The sad reality is that in this country there are an unfathomable number of people who graduate high school and even college without ever having received the help they needed.

And that's where John's story comes in.

John faced the profound challenge of concealing his illiteracy while building a career in education. He was a teacher in the California school system for seventeen years yet could not read!

He told me stories of how he learned to navigate intimidating school situations to avoid being "found out." When the teacher would call on him to read, he created chaos by being disruptive so that soon his behavior stole attention away from his academic challenges.

He remorsefully shared that he had cheated his way through college, once stealing a file cabinet out of a professor's office to get the answers to all the tests. He stole an *entire* file cabinet, lugged it to his house, called a locksmith to make him a copy of the key to it, and then put it back. Imagine going to those dangerous lengths just to conceal a secret, hide your shame, and try to fit in.

John went on to become a highly successful businessman and millionaire, but he didn't learn to read until age forty-eight.

And no one noticed.

I knew this was a story I needed to tell, so I decided to secure support for a movie called *The Truth About Reading*. The reality is we all likely know someone who is subliterate and struggles to get through their workday. Remember, 60 percent of America fits this description!

How many kids are sitting in class right now sweating and ashamed and terrified to participate? How many kids will graduate and have to face life with a painful secret and massive disadvantage?

Maybe that woman at work that everyone says is so quiet has brilliant ideas but has learned that flying under the radar will prevent her from being the butt of jokes.

These are the kinds of stories I told people when I was asking for support for the film.

I know that true stories about real people are a force capable of breaking down barriers, dismantling prejudices, and saving lives.

Whatever your goal is, there is likely a human component to it. Find it.

Tell the story your audience hasn't heard.

Tell the one that cuts right through to their hearts and their desire to be a force for good in the world. Tell them stories that make common sense but are not a part of their common knowledge.

Persuasion Changes Lives

My journey has taught me that while closing deals may offer momentary triumphs, the real success of any venture is in the relationships built through persuading someone to join your team.

It is the antidote to apathy and ignorance.

In a world teeming with diverse perspectives, the power to

persuade becomes a bridge that closes the gaps between our differences and creates pathways for partnership and progress.

I believe that my purpose in life is to tell stories that drive change. I know of people who have chosen to stay alive after watching one of our films. I know of people who have left unfulfilling jobs to chase lifelong dreams after watching one of our films. And those two reasons alone are enough for me to tell these stories for the rest of my life.

I feel so lucky to do what I do, and sometimes I think about those people and how drastically different their lives might have gone had I not listened to others' perspectives, joined their team, shared my passion for their missions, and persuaded people to help me make these films.

It doesn't matter if you don't consider yourself a great speaker. It doesn't matter if you're an introvert who hates addressing a crowd. When you are serving a cause that lights you up, you don't need to sell it.

You simply need to gather up all your enthusiasm, your passion, and your desire and transfer it to your listeners with a true and powerful story.

In business, persuasion is the needle that stitches together world-changing ideas and fuels our commitment to significant causes.

It's the quiet force that amplifies our voice and unlocks the door to a reality where meaningful change is not just sought after but *realized*.

And for me, it's the powerful and trusty sidekick that's allowed me to live out my wildest dreams and fulfill my purpose in life. I know it will unlock a whole world of possibilities for you too. When it does, be sure to let me know!

About Nick

From the slums of Port-au-Prince, Haiti, with special forces raiding a sex trafficking ring and freeing children, to the Virgin Galactic Space Port in Mojave with Sir Richard Branson, twenty-two-time Emmy Award–winning Director-Producer Nick Nanton has become known for telling stories that connect. Why? Because he focuses on the most fascinating subject in the world: *people*. As an award-winning songwriter, storyteller, and best-selling author, Nick has shared his message with millions of people through his documentaries, speeches, blogs, lectures, songs, and best-selling books. Nick's book *StorySelling* hit The Wall Street Journal Best-Seller List and is available on Audible as an audiobook. Nick has directed more than sixty documentaries and a sold-out Broadway Show (garnering forty-three Emmy nominations in multiple regions and twenty-two wins), including:

- *DICKIE V* (ESPN/Disney+)
- *Rudy Ruettiger: The Walk On* (Amazon Prime)
- *The Rebound* (Netflix)
- *Operation Toussaint* (Amazon Prime)

Nick has shared the stage with, coauthored books with, and made films featuring:

- Larry King
- Kathie Lee Gifford
- Hoda Kotb
- Dick Vitale
- Kenny Chesney
- Magic Johnson
- Coach Mike Krzyzewski
- Jack Nicklaus
- Tony Robbins
- Lisa Nichols
- Peter Diamandis
- And many more

Nick specializes in bringing the element of human connection to every viewer, no matter the subject. He is currently directing and hosting the series *In Case You Didn't Know* (season 1 executive produced by Larry King), featuring legends in the worlds of business, entrepreneurship, personal development, technology, and sports.

Nick's first love has always been music. He has been writing songs for more than two decades, and his songs have been aired on radio across the United States and in Canada. He is currently ranked in the top 10 percent of songwriters in the world. His songs have been recorded by Lee Brice, Darius Rucker, RaeLynn, Joe Bryson, and many more, and have amassed more than three million streams on Spotify, Apple Music, Pandora, and SoundCloud. He received three Gold records in 2018 for his work with the global touring band A Day to Remember.

Nick has written and/or produced songs that have appeared on the following shows or in promotional commercials for:

- the Fox prime-time series *Glee, New Girl, House,* and *Hell's Kitchen*
- the MLB All-Star Game
- ABC Family's hit series *Falcon Beach*
- the CBS prime-time series *Ghost Whisperer* starring Jennifer Love Hewitt

CHAPTER 10

MAKING AN IMPACT BY BECOMING THE CEO OF YOUR OWN LIFE!

By Joe White

"We're going to have to let you go."

I swallowed hard and stared ahead of me, too stunned to say anything. Had I heard that correctly? The air seemed to be sucked out of the room. A minute before the phone rang, I was reviewing my student's work and contentedly planning my next lesson, and now I was frozen where I stood, the heaviness of what this meant bearing down on me.

Just eight words had totally shattered the security I thought I had built.

You see, in Ontario the public sector has what's referred to as the Sunshine List. This is a list of people who've made more than $100,000 the previous year. And I would have been on that list because I'd been developing courses and working nonstop for long hours, outside of my regular duties, racking up billable hours. I loved it because it was my passion. But that list is published and made public, and unfortunately, the college didn't want me on it. So my employment was "paused," full stop, midyear.

I get it. People lose their jobs all the time. And while I understood that it was just business, it felt like a betrayal, like a punch in the gut.

That year was 2008. I'd entered the mortgage brokering industry in the late '80s, when I was in my early twenties. When I took the mortgage brokering course at Seneca College, my instructor said the industry was growing, and he needed a TA for the next semester. I didn't know how it would benefit me at the time, but I thought that if I could get in front of people coming into this industry, those who would eventually be leaders, how could it hurt? The industry was good to me. I found a mentor who took me under his wing and taught me what I needed to know to be successful.

I did so well that I was offered a position teaching that course while simultaneously working in the industry. Then, over time, I was offered the opportunity to run the fourteen-course program. I embraced the challenge. By then, in the late '90s, I was developing courses for the program, hiring instructors, managing the program, and running a team of mortgage agents for a national brokerage. I had an opportunity to write the textbook for the mortgage agent course. I did it! I'd never undertaken anything like that before, but I kept grabbing these opportunities and running with them.

I was doing what I loved, and I loved what I was doing.

But I'd never had a plan. That was obvious; I hadn't seen the "pause" coming. I had been lucky enough to enjoy a steady flow of opportunities. Then, that fateful day in 2008 shattered the illusion of that security.

It was then that I learned I needed my own plan. I needed to run my own life. It was time to become the CEO of my life by becoming the CEO of a new company.

I immediately incorporated a new company, and I called it REMIC, the Real Estate and Mortgage Institute of Canada. My plan was to build a company that would cross over into both the real estate and mortgage industries. I'd leverage my now well-known name in the industry to compete with my former employer. And I did.

Eventually, Seneca discontinued the course. They didn't have enough students. REMIC had a 75 percent market share. We had other competitors, but my plan was to develop the most complete program in the industry, aggressively market it, and dominate the industry.

This is what happens when you refuse to be beaten down and decide instead to become CEO of your own life.

LIFE IS LIKE A BUSINESS PLAN

REMIC had twelve thousand students this year. It's hugely rewarding to witness people's lives transform because of our programs.

Most of the time when new students come to us, they are driven by a goal of creating better lives for themselves and their families.

Our program is an opportunity for them to take control of their lives, become their own bosses, and build the lifestyle they want. The success stories are the fuel that keeps me and my entire team going. Our students have gone on to achieve great successes, running brokerages and changing their lives for the better.

But I started to notice something.

I would watch some of our students, who had done exceptionally well in our program, struggle in the "real world."

What I realized is that they were leaving with technical knowledge but had no clue how to actually build a business or structure their lives around it. The ones who were successful were quite often like me years ago—grabbing hold of opportunities and running with them. But finding an opportunity and grabbing hold of it is not a plan. It's not scalable. It's not something that I could teach.

Many didn't know how to set goals and projections. They didn't know how to differentiate themselves in the market or build affiliate partnerships. They didn't know how to balance the hustle of getting clients with the juggling of family life.

My goal was, and is, to change that. I'm here to provide a road map for success well beyond the classroom and encourage each of them to become CEO of their own life.

And CEOs make business plans.

It's Groundhog Day... Again

If you've never seen the movie *Groundhog Day* with Bill Murray, let me sum it up for you. It's the story of a cynical TV reporter who is assigned to cover the events of Groundhog Day in Punxsutawney, Pennsylvania. Somehow he gets stuck in a time loop and is forced to live that same day over and over again.

I came to realize that most of us are stuck in Groundhog Day.

We get up, brush our teeth, go to work, push paper around, sit in meetings, go home, eat dinner, sleep, and then get up and do it all over again.

Most of the time, we are so stuck in that routine that we give little thought to how we might like our day to go instead.

Life is an ecosystem where careers and personal lives live, intertwined.

We can't run a successful business if our personal lives are falling apart, and we can't relax into great relationships if we are drowning in debt and our careers are in the toilet.

All the facets of our lives feed each other.

Before I started my company, I used to manage a team of more than one hundred agents. I ran an exercise in sales training around the concept of building the perfect day. I invited them to picture themselves as a business owner and picture their most profitable employee. I then prompted them to map out that person's day hour by hour. When do they get up? Where do they go? Whom do they call? What time do they leave work? How do they use their free time?

Most people had an obvious idea of how they thought a successful person should run their day.

Then I asked them to write down, hour by hour, how they currently run their own days. It was jarring.

Many of them realized that they weren't doing a fraction of the things they felt a successful person would do.

How would they run a business if they weren't walking the

walk? Who would trust them to lead? Who would respect them if they were doing *less* than their employees?

Just as a profitable business requires planning and leadership, so do our lives.

An intelligent manager will set goals, measure progress, and learn from setbacks. Why not apply those same principles of success to our own lives?

Imagine the impact we could have on ourselves, our families, and the world if we actually woke up every day and lived with intention.

You can have all the proper education and be surrounded by five-star opportunities, but if you're managing your life more like an apathetic employee than a driven leader, you could stay stuck in Groundhog Day forever.

You Can't Manage Anything Until You Can Manage Yourself

Let's talk about the core aspects of a well-thought-out business plan and the role that plan should play in the success of a business.

As author Simon Sinek suggests, it should start with a *why*.

- It should have clear and measurable goals.

- It should have concrete action steps for how those goals will be achieved.

- It should have a forward-looking budget and other financial controls.

- It should contain a list of resources necessary for the business to run.

And it should spell out what will happen if the plan is followed—namely, the profit and total owner benefits.

Let's start with a mission.

The mission of my business is to transform students into

entrepreneurs. It is a personal and professional mission. That *why* gives me a barometer to measure against. Every course we create, every person we hire, either supports that mission statement or it doesn't. And if it doesn't, it goes.

Imagine how much easier it would be to make decisions if all you had to do was weigh your options against your *why*.

If you're having trouble connecting to any kind of purposeful *why*, it's time for a *"why* check."

I've asked a couple of students over the years why they want to own their businesses, and I always bristle a little when they say, "To make as much money as I can."

Is that a real *why*? Of course not. It's too vague. Drill down. Is it to put your kids through college? Buy your dream house? Plan for retirement? You need to know the exact reasons so you'll have the motivation to get up every morning. Because if you don't know your real *why*, or *whys*, you'll always find a real reason to stay in bed, to try a little less hard, to let those opportunities slip through your fingers.

When we begin with managing ourselves through the lens of a business plan that is built on a solid core *why*, we have a much better shot at a great ROI.

Failure to Launch: Lessons Learned

The Ontario Science Center was bustling with activity. My partners and I had orchestrated a launch party for our new product, CAIT, which stands for conversational artificial intelligence technologies. This was five years ago. Amazon had just come out with its first bot, so AI was fairly new. Our technology was cutting-edge, and we believed we were on the precipice of something huge.

We invited Canadian astronaut Chris Hadfield to provide opening remarks and made sure there was plenty of media coverage. If you were there, you would have felt as if you were witnessing the start of something extraordinary.

Unfortunately, from that moment forward we ran into a brick wall. Zero ROI.

What happened?

I would love to blame the industry or the economy. But the truth is, while we had plans for how to create the product, we didn't have enough of a plan for what should happen once the product was created. We hadn't positioned it properly. We hadn't educated the market enough. We got high on our own PR and were so distracted by the excitement that we didn't do the actual research, which would have shown that most companies wouldn't know how to incorporate this technology into their daily operations.

It was a key persuasion tactic we had totally missed—you can't influence anyone until you take the time to find out what they want and need.

We gave ourselves twelve months to turn it around, and when it didn't, we pulled the plug.

I was devastated because it could have had a huge impact on the world and instead, it had no impact at all.

It did, however, have an impact on me.

It reminded me of what we teach our students. Build a solid plan, not just for the launch but the application. Be clear about what you want from your life or business in one year, five years, and ten. Learn from your mistakes.

And perhaps most importantly, be honest with yourself. Sometimes the most well-intended plans need to go back to the drawing board...or in the trash.

What's Your UVP?

When I taught at Seneca College, I ran a course on starting a business, and one of the requirements was that each student write a business plan. I required them to do market research on the other brokerages in the industry. I wanted them to tell me why they were going to succeed. They returned with common answers, mostly lifted from the taglines of other companies.

I pointed out that if they went to the market that day with those answers, they would be out of business in a month! I wanted them to figure out why their businesses were different and competitive. I wanted them to find their *unique value proposition*.

But being unique is more difficult than it sounds. It means sacrificing. It means being willing to live a couple of years as most people *won't* so you can live the rest of your life as most people *can't*.

You must know your unique value proposition and what you specifically bring to the table, and then be able to communicate that to the market. The same is true for life. We've all got to take time to know ourselves and what unique gifts we have to offer the world.

Many people know exactly what they have to offer; the problem is they don't. I can't imagine where I would be today if I had zeroed in on my gift, which is to teach, and zeroed in on my purpose, which is to transform students into entrepreneurs, and then ignored both of those things and took a job working for someone else where I couldn't experience either.

Actually, I can imagine it, and it's pretty dismal!

The guy who waited on me at lunch two years ago and ended up going through our school and becoming a successful broker might still be waiting tables.

The taxi driver who came to us because he wanted more for his family might still be struggling to make ends meet.

Just as any idea needs a business plan to champion it into existence, your gifts (and the people who benefit from them) need *you* to give them oxygen. Envision the life and career you want, and map out a plan that helps you get it.

Regardless of where you are while you're reading this, you can choose to pivot, relaunch, and lead yourself in a new direction. Whether you're looking for a change or struggling in a dead-end job, you now have an opportunity all your own.

Be the CEO of your own life.

About Joe

Joe White, a visionary leader and best-selling author, has devoted thirty-five years to empowering entrepreneurs in the financial services sector. As a celebrated educator and trainer, Joe's profound influence is reflected in the success of over sixty thousand copies of his books sold worldwide, each designed to enhance the potential of aspiring business leaders.

As the founder, president, and CEO of the Real Estate and Mortgage Institute of Canada (REMIC), Joe has shaped industry standards since 2008, building on his significant experience as the former head of the mortgage broker program at Ontario's largest college. His expertise and leadership were formally recognized in 2019 when he was inducted into the Canadian Mortgage Hall of Fame, a testament to his impact and dedication to the field.

Furthering his commitment to integrity and excellence, Joe established the Association of Mortgage Investment Professionals (AMIPROS) and the Fraud Prevention Centre of Canada (FPCC). These organizations underscore his dedication to nurturing a thriving environment for professionals and championing national efforts in fraud prevention and awareness.

In 2024 Joe launched *The Billion Dollar Podcast*, a dynamic platform where he shares innovative strategies that transcend industry boundaries, helping individuals achieve remarkable success and make a significant impact on their communities and beyond.

Residing in the Greater Toronto area with his family, Joe continues to inspire change and drive progress within the financial sector. He is accessible for further insights and collaboration via email at joe.white@remic.ca.

CHAPTER 11

TRUSTING YOURSELF TO LEAD...EVEN AFTER LIFE FALLS APART

By Elizabeth Rowe

The car idled in the parking lot, the hum of the engine cutting through the tense silence.

I was shaken to my core, stunned at the shocking confession.

Her words hung in the air like a heavy cloud pressing down and crushing me with the realization that this betrayal had happened right under my nose. My assistant had embezzled tens of thousands of dollars from me. It's a strange and numbing feeling, being conned by someone you trust, a cocktail blend of anger, sadness, shame, and disillusionment.

Our relationship was not just professional; it was personal. After I hired her, I had given her responsibilities and coached her in financial literacy.

She had become a part of my life, even acting as a night nanny for my new baby. The revelation that someone I considered a friend had been stealing from me unfolded like a slow-motion catastrophe.

Looking back now, I'm not surprised that her actions had gone unnoticed. I was drowning.

She threw a life raft.

I grabbed it and didn't let go.

THE MESSAGE IS IN THE MIDDLE

A lot of people tell the beginning and the end of their stories, painting a tidy picture of before and after their success. For me, the middle of my story became the place where I learned the most lessons.

Today, I am the principal broker and owner of Rowe Real Estate, a full-service real estate firm that offers residential, commercial, and property management services.

Just a few short years ago, however, following that betrayal, I was suffering from PTSD and contemplating suicide.

The years leading up to that had been incredibly challenging.

I was navigating a tumultuous marriage that was draining the life out of me. My husband at the time struggled with alcoholism, and I felt totally abandoned and overwhelmed. While I was excited to meet my baby, the weight of the dysfunction in my relationship bore down on me, casting a shadow over what should have been the happiest time of my life.

I bought the clothes and painted the nursery, giddily anticipating the light this little being would bring into our lives. Nothing could have prepared me for what happened next.

I had no idea that I would nearly die trying to bring this baby into the world, but that's exactly what happened.

My son was blue. The umbilical cord was wrapped around his neck. My blood pressure dropped to 60/20, and the last thing I remember was hearing a bucket of blood hit the floor.

The medical team moved with urgency and saved my life, but I was left traumatized by the whole experience.

So of course, I readily accepted my assistant's offer to be my night nanny so I could sleep and heal. She felt like a true partner, something I felt I didn't have at that time. I knew things at the office were slipping through my fingers, but she never hesitated to reassure me that things would be OK. Everything I panicked about was met with a reassuring, "Don't worry, Elizabeth. I'll handle it."

I remember regularly checking the account and thinking, "Wow, with as much as we had been closing, there should be more money in here!" I asked her about it, but she always had an answer that made sense.

Has that ever happened to you—the universe sends you a sign that you've been asleep at the wheel, but you're so tired, so desperate for a life raft that you look away, needing to believe that someone, anyone, has your back?

That was me at that time.

After the embezzlement, I was terribly depressed. I would tell my husband that I was going to work, but instead, I'd drive to an empty parking lot and sleep all day in the third row of my SUV, and the business was crumbling. One day, after another eight hours spent sleeping in my car outside a grocery store, I remembered something my mother used to say: "You can't be powerful if you're pitiful." I knew in that moment, I had to pull myself out of this.

And I did. One. Step. At a time.

I hired a new assistant to help me get back to work and returned to my office for the first time in months. My new assistant could sense that the office was dredging up terrible memories for me and said, "Well, this just won't do. Come on, we're going to find a new office." There was a beautiful space I had dreamed of getting into, and as luck would have it, there was a "For Lease" sign out front. We signed a lease.

I was scared, but my mother had always said, *"I don't care that you're scared...just do it scared!"*

And that's when it occurred to me that sometimes the person you need to persuade and influence the most is yourself.

PERMISSION TO START OVER...AGAIN AND AGAIN

Real estate was never part of my career plan. I started out as a biology major at the University of Arkansas. It wasn't until the summer after my sophomore year that my friends and I were looking for a place to rent and decided to call an agent.

At our first appointment he said, "You really command attention when you speak. Have you ever thought about a career in real estate?"

He suggested I come and work for his office for the summer just to make some extra money. I eagerly tagged along to my first closing with a sweet family to hand them the keys to their new house. They had a new baby and were so grateful and excited. I thought, "I can make this much of a difference in people's lives, be in a competitive environment, *and* make *how* much money? Sign me up!"

Fifteen credits short of a bachelor's degree in biology, I decided to become a real estate agent instead.

Now, I absolutely love what I do, and this career has provided an amazing life for my family. But I wouldn't be doing it had I not permitted myself to change course right before the finish line.

I started over back then.

I started over after the embezzlement.

And I'll probably start over ten more times in my life.

I used to look at starting over as a failure. Now I see starting over as one of the privileges of being alive.

PERMISSION TO LEAD

Standing on the weathered front porch of a beat-up rural Arkansas home, I seriously contemplated my life's choices. A friend, who happened to be an attorney, had connected me with her client—a couple embroiled in a nasty divorce and desperate to off-load their property and run from each other as fast as they could.

The home was a *disaster*. Imagine an alcoholic drug addict who decided to DIY a remodel on the interior of the home. Most projects were left undone. Insulation hung from the ceilings and walls. The countertops in the kitchen looked as if they were sourced remnants from the dumpster behind Lowe's, as nothing matched.

It smelled *terrible*. They attempted a bathroom remodel at some point and cut into the wall, hitting a vented plumbing pipe that let sewer gas fill the house.

The sellers, a woman who referred to herself as Sexy Jenn and a man named Billy Bob, couldn't stand each other, and I wondered how I could bill them for being both their Realtor and their therapist! Every interaction between them was triggering and uncomfortable. So, there I was, caught in the middle, trying to get these two to see eye to eye on selling their less-than-desirable property, but it was like trying to wrangle a pair of stubborn mules. Every time we made progress, they would rehash old arguments and point fingers.

I had to dig deep into my toolbox for some patience and empathy!

When they would lash out in anger, yelling various accusations into the phone at me, I would employ tactical empathy by labeling their feelings, mirroring them, and then summarizing their frustrations. Instead of brushing aside their emotions, I actively listened to their concerns and empathized with their experiences. By demonstrating true empathy, I built rapport and trust with Sexy Jenn and Billy Bob, creating a conducive environment for constructive dialogue.

And it paid off. Despite their differences, I was able to negotiate a deal and get their house sold before it went to auction. They were both able to walk away with money in their pockets and use it to start new lives... separately!

Real estate is an emotional business. Agents might look at a property closing transactionally, but our clients are looking at the growth chart on their kitchen wall and remembering exactly what their child looked like standing there—or they're seeing the home as a card to play in a bitter divorce.

What I have found is that the most successful interactions are driven not by dollars and cents but by empathy.

In any negotiation letting go of the numbers and making a true effort to understand the emotional components is a much more effective strategy for cultivating collaboration and closing a deal that everyone can feel good about.

PERMISSION TO GET QUIET

Since I was a young girl, fly-fishing has been my favorite hobby. When I'm standing in the water with the sun on my face, casting my line, I'm not thinking about the meeting I had that morning, the conversation I need to have that night, or the conflict happening in a transaction. My mind is quiet. It's ironic that not thinking leads to my best thinking.

That's the flow state!

If you're not familiar with the flow state, it's a state of being completely absorbed in a task, directing all of your attention to it and entering "the zone." In "the zone" there is no self-consciousness, no judgment, no disruptive thoughts, and in the absence of those things, clarity has room to come through.

We need to get quiet...and humans are terrible at that.

After all, there is always so much to do. So much to worry about.

If we're not careful, we run the risk of being so busy and so distracted that we fail to recognize the sound of our own inner voice.

Looking back, I realize now that that's what happened to me.

When I was going through IVF, when I was working sixty-to-eighty-hour weeks, when my assistant was stealing from me, guess how many times I went fly-fishing!

Zero!

We live in a hustle culture that labels rest as laziness. But getting quiet is an act of productivity. Studies show that people are approximately 30 percent more cognitively creative when they are in a relaxed and positive state of mind.

Therefore, rest is an active practice that allows you to reflect and to enter a dialog with your own inner wisdom.

So give yourself permission to step away from the noise.

In the quiet, you might get a new business idea, solve a contract problem, or realize that the knot in your stomach is trying to tell you that your assistant is wrecking your life!

I can't help but wonder, if I had given myself permission to rest and get quiet during all that, if I would have heard the voice of my intuition whispering to me.

And it might have saved me a whole lot of heartache.

Permission to Let Go

"Do you know who this is?"

There was silence on the other end of the line for what felt like an eternity.

Then finally, a very timid, "Yes. I know who this is."

Twelve months had passed since my assistant had confessed her embezzlement, and I hadn't spoken to her or laid eyes on her since. Over those twelve months, I had imagined all kinds of terrible scenarios and plotted out several versions of my revenge until I realized that my rage was distracting me from the one thing I had been determined to do: *live*.

So that morning, which was her birthday, I decided to call.

"I just want you to know that I forgive you," I said. "I'm not going to prosecute. You don't have to keep looking over your shoulder for me."

I hung up the phone, and the burden lifted from my shoulders. In that moment, despite having every justification for being angry, I had to persuade myself to let go.

Sometimes the most powerful impact comes from knowing when to step back.

I couldn't focus on growth if my eyes were focused on revenge. I had already been robbed; I wasn't about to let bitterness steal from me too. Think about all the things we let distract us from our mission.

Sometimes our fear distracts us from our knowledge.

Sometimes our ego distracts us from our empathy.

Whatever your goal is, it needs your focus. You've got to be willing to let go of anything that's pulling your attention away.

Business is booming, my kids are thriving, and life is very full. But my arms couldn't hold all that success if they were still holding all that resentment.

A ROOM WITH A VIEW

A few weeks ago I walked into the office and let out a long exhale. The sun was shining through the floor-to-ceiling windows. I used to drive by this office building, look in these windows, and think, "*That's* what success looks like!"

Now I'm on the inside of that building looking out, proof that taking consistent, small steps can lead to big things.

I use persuasive communication every day in my work.

But I use my persuasive skills the most on my own mind.

Persuasion and permission are partners.

Before you can have an impact on anything, you've got to give yourself permission to evolve, to pivot, to speak up, to get quiet, to lead.

After all, you can't influence anyone else until you learn to influence yourself!

About Elizabeth

Elizabeth Rowe is a dynamic force in the world of real estate, having seamlessly woven together her small-town roots with a visionary approach to business and life.

At the tender age of twenty, Elizabeth embarked on her real estate career—a bold leap into the unknown that would set the stage for her future success.

In 2012 Elizabeth took a leap of faith and opened her own company, Rowe Real Estate. Under her leadership, Rowe Real Estate flourished, becoming a beacon of excellence in the Northwest Arkansas community.

A pivotal moment in Elizabeth's journey came in 2006 when she crossed paths with Buffini & Co., a renowned coaching company that would forever change the trajectory of her career. With their guidance and support, Elizabeth unlocked new levels of success, leveraging their proven strategies to propel her business forward.

In addition to her thriving business ventures, Elizabeth finds immense fulfillment in coaching new real estate agents, sharing her knowledge and expertise to empower others to achieve their goals. It's a role she cherishes, knowing that she's making a tangible difference in the lives of aspiring professionals.

Elizabeth's accolades speak volumes about her impact on the industry, from being recognized as Fayetteville's Chamber Woman-Owned Business of the Year in 2020 to her greatest accomplishment—being a devoted mother to two boys. Her philosophy is simple: If it's funny, you're not in trouble—a lighthearted approach to parenting that reflects her warmth and humor.

Outside of work, Elizabeth is a force of nature, channeling her boundless energy into pursuits such as fly-fishing, hiking, camping, and other outdoor adventures.

As the host of *The Rowe Report*, Elizabeth shares her insights and expertise with a global audience, guiding agents to fiscal responsibility, relationship building, and an unwavering commitment to excellence.

In Elizabeth Rowe we find not just a real estate maven but a beacon of inspiration—a testament to the transformative power of passion, perseverance, and the relentless pursuit of excellence.

CHAPTER 12

NEGOTIATIONS IN AN ANONYMOUS WORLD

By Dmitry Mishunin

bet you were deceived at least once in your life.

Perhaps it was an unfair merchant who kept a portion of your change, or your friend who borrowed money from you and never paid it back.

You know this feeling. I do too. There isn't a human on this earth who hasn't felt the pain of deception at least once.

The structure of deception is rooted in our instinctual need to protect ourselves.

We deceive by concealing information or presenting false versions of it or by misrepresenting facts.

In today's digitally driven world, one of the most common forms of deception is impersonation. Every day we hear stories of people entangled with someone they met on the internet, only to find out that they were interacting with someone who had created a totally false identity.

Where does that leave us?

How do we do business in a world that's made it increasingly easier to lie and manipulate outcomes?

Is it even possible to negotiate when the person on the other side is an anonymous avatar with a false name and a cartoon profile picture? Yes.

And since that is where the world is heading, it's time to learn how.

TRUSTLESS ENVIRONMENTS

Let's imagine a trustless environment, which is designed especially for operations where no one trusts each other. We already have such systems. Some of these systems are called blockchains. Blockchains are designed in such a way to make every operation transparent and provide no opportunity for fraud.

Contrary to popular belief, the term *trustless*, doesn't imply that trust is absent.

What it means is that trust is redistributed away from centralized authorities to decentralized networks. While trust in individuals or institutions may be minimized, trust in the integrity and security of the technology and protocols is essential. Therefore, a trustless environment doesn't mean that "no one can be trusted"; rather, it means trust is placed in the technology, rather than in any single entity.

In contrast, in centralized systems such as storing money in a bank account, all the trust is placed on one party (the bank).

While we won't dive into the blockchain topic itself, as that could be its own separate book, we will still dive into the heads of its creators. Even the best trustless systems are designed and created by humans.

In fact, it would be difficult to find any system, software, or community that can't be traced back to a human.

That's good news for us. Where there is a human, there's the potential for negotiating!

NOTHING IS WHAT IT SEEMS

We live in a world of profile pictures, avatars, and nicknames.

Spend ten minutes googling, and you'll figure out how to get a fake passport, a fake driver's license, and even fake degrees.

Google "internet scams," and there are nearly 1.5 billion search results.

This pervasive dishonesty perpetuated by the ability to hide behind a screen leaves us with two choices: Do nothing because we are afraid of getting scammed, or figure out how to conduct business with people we can't see and sometimes people whose existence we can't even prove.

Obviously, we need to keep moving forward, and that means we must cultivate the skill of paying close attention to indications of a scam and learn to develop our own instincts.

One time a company requested an audit from us, and though we never met them, they portrayed themselves well. During the audit, we discovered that the project could function as a Ponzi scheme. Despite this, the source code was solid. They had anticipated a favorable report from us; however, we included a warning in the report, cautioning that the code could be utilized in a Ponzi scheme and urging users to pay close attention.

Often we allow clients time to address any issues outlined in the report. Once the updates are completed, we proceed with publication. This time, however, the situation unfolded differently. Instead of rectifying the code, they shared only the first page of our report on their social media platforms. It was a title page with no content! They deceived their users.

At that point, we could have gotten scared and decided to only do business with people we could actually see and talk to... but as the next project would prove, that would have been a big mistake!

The Role of Empathy in Impersonal Negotiations

There is a misguided school in business that emails and text messages are the key to efficient communication.

It takes less time and energy to send a text than to schedule a meeting.

The problem with this is that during a conversation, at least 70 percent of information is transferred via nonverbal channels such as emotions, tone of voice, and body language.

Just imagine that you've received a letter that is burned by fire.

You need to decrypt information on a burnt page, except only a few letters remain intact.

Virtually impossible, right? That's how anonymous communication works. Two people are trying to speak with each other, transmitting only 30 percent of the information they have.

Every day, at least 50 percent of the requests that come into my company are anonymous, and I have to try to figure out the missing pieces of information.

When I cannot see the other party, my personal decryptor is tactical empathy and its instruments.

Empathy plays a vital role in the impersonal world of anonymity.

Once I got a chat request from a guy called "rugdaddy" with a bull on his profile pic. I thought, "Not very original. I've seen this avatar a hundred times!"

It's difficult to work with an anon—you never know their real motivation. You don't see them, don't know how they are feeling, and can't tell if they are lying.

"Hey! I need an audit," he said.

I hesitantly replied, "OK, I'll need some details. Please share the source code with us. Also, I would like to know how you found out about us."

"I liked your website," he said matter-of-factly.

Really? Who chooses an auditor based on their website? That caught me off guard, so I knew I needed to dig deeper. I started a dialog unrelated to the request itself. I asked about his experience, challenges he faced, and he described the pains of missed deadlines and incorrect deliverables. I had felt his pain many times, and I shared some professional anecdotes with him. We "got" each other.

In the end this opened a huge opportunity for us as "rugdaddy" turned out to be a highly influential person in the industry. We became partners, and to this day we collaborate on many profitable projects.

Imagine losing an incredible opportunity simply because the person on the other side of the screen is anonymous! The key is to deploy empathy and attempt to understand the human behind the avatar.

Many leaders choose to act like automated response services rather than people. That attitude stands in the way of properly reacting to incoming information. The real motivation is always hidden behind a facade, and our job is to break through it and reach for the true image of a person. Being empathetic is a big part of that.

TACTICS FOR NEGOTIATION IN AN ANONYMOUS WORLD

Let's clarify one crucial thing. Being empathetic is not the same as being emotional. While the former quality is focused on building trust and understanding, the latter leads to irrational decision-making. The two can't work together. A clear mind is required to be empathetic.

While anonymous negotiations have their drawbacks, there are benefits. It's easier to remain calm, pause for contemplation, and respond objectively in a messenger. A classy demeanor is more achievable from behind the screen, and the self-control techniques that serve well during real-life negotiations can be left aside.

Regardless of whether I can see the other person, following are some of the tools I use to facilitate a successful outcome.

Labeling: Don't feel their pain. Label it! Labeling is assigning a word or phrase to the other party's perspectives to validate their feelings. If you feel that they are pushing you and you want to reduce tension, you might say, "It seems like you're a responsible person and this project is really valuable for you."

Mirroring: Mirroring involves repeating the last few words spoken by the other party to encourage further elaboration and to show that you are actively listening.

Asking calibrated questions: Calibrated questions are carefully curated questions designed to gather information but also to guide the negotiation in the direction you want it to go. Instead of bargaining, try asking, "How am I supposed to do this?" or, "How should we approach this?" Then pause and wait for the other side to begin solving the problem. From now on they're playing for your team.

Summarizing and paraphrasing: When you summarize the other party's words, it shows that you are listening and attempting to understand. It also removes the possibility of confusion or any retractions later.

Getting a "that's right": "That's right" usually means that the other side feels understood. A yes generally means nothing.

Mastering no: In negotiations a no instead of a yes is your best friend. When people say no, they show their boundaries. This helps foster a safer atmosphere; when each side knows and expresses each other's boundaries, it's harder to get hurt. When anon throws a "that company does it cheaper" at you, say, "I apologize, but we can't afford it at this time."

If the deal seems risky or lacks integrity, be prepared to reject it. If you have a gut feeling, trust it. Many times my instincts have saved me from wasting time, losing money, and even getting in trouble.

Finally, remember that nothing said or proposed in a chat is a personal attack. Everyone at the negotiation table, virtual or real, has only one goal in mind: getting the best possible outcome.

Empathy in Community Management

Every business today is online. It's not just a website anymore; to successfully function, you need to have social networks, a messenger channel, or a forum.

That forms a community. The main difference is that in an online community, anonymous users can actively participate. Their anonymity allows for any action without repercussions. Today the community affects the success of a product as much as its shareholders.

If you want your business to flourish in this new reality, you must learn to interact with the community. We learned the hard way.

We had decided to create our own community-based project. We launched with highly strategic marketing and onboarded two thousand people in less than twenty-four hours. Seems like a success, right?

Wrong!

Every day, I woke up with hundreds of messages. Users weren't happy. They had questions and needed to constantly be in communication with us.

We hired support staff, who gave us some breathing room.

We worked 24/7, and still people complained.

No matter how much we gave, they wanted more. But we had no more, so eventually, the community declined. We made so many mistakes with its management—even great profits couldn't keep the boat afloat.

Here's what we learned:

Communities might be anonymous by nature, but the members are still *human*!

Always share both failures and issues. Don't just announce successes. Humans don't like perfect things—we feel imperfect next to them and instinctively search for imperfections. And those who seek always find.

Remain open and honest. You can't satisfy everyone, but you can keep your conscience clean.

Nobody really cares about your road map. Everyone has their own goals in mind.

Share updates and deadlines cautiously. People's expectations and imaginary profits will depend on them. We shot ourselves in the foot by sharing something way too early. Our goal was to get people excited, but when deadlines were not met, our news turned into memes used against us.

Don't be afraid to seek advice. Humans enjoy being engaged in collective efforts. We are social creatures, and it's one of our needs to participate in a social group.

That said, don't apply community ideas right away. Occasionally, we tried to quickly implement community suggestions. However, often the ideas were useless for the project. One thing we must never forget is that as leaders, we are responsible for everything. It's not the community that will be held accountable, so the final decision cannot come from them; it comes from you.

Community quality is more important than size.

It's better to have a cult following of five hundred users who actively use your product and generate product growth than lure in thirty thousand freeloaders and bots who don't actually care. Keep in mind that even if you grow your cult following to 5K, you'll have to be sure you aren't biting off more than you can chew.

FUD CONTROL IS VITAL

You have to be careful in managing FUD, which is the spread of fear, uncertainty, and doubt usually aimed to undermine the community itself, its leadership team, or its initiatives.

People are impressionable. If FUD is allowed to run uncontrolled, it won't be long before you find yourself with a completely dissatisfied and angry community, attacking you for simply trying to lead with truth.

You can bring the banhammer or engage in a verbal duel, but it won't matter after the damage has already been done.

TROLL CONTROL IS A TOP PRIORITY

Since online communities are based on anonymity, they're a perfect breeding ground for the worst kinds of users. Things can go downhill fast in a chat when users start posting inappropriate comments. Before you manage to delete them, people will join in, because anonymity absolves from consequences.

An entire community can be degraded and corrupted in a matter of hours.

People in such situations tend to succumb to mob mentality.

Best-case scenario—your followers act like a pack of "wolves" and jump at any chance to defend your project from both FUD and trolls. Learning how to handle your community can be your biggest nightmare or greatest shield.

Treat members with respect and listen to their needs, but set clear boundaries that cultivate a positive and productive environment.

Systems Run the World, but People Run the Systems

We're living in a digital world with a vast anonymous landscape. While that has changed the technology through which we conduct business, it shouldn't change the skills we use to facilitate successful outcomes.

No matter how many innovations are born over the next few years, or how robust the software becomes, human beings will remain at the root of every business interaction.

Even in the virtual world, where teams work remotely and avatars hide identities, negotiation and relationship building are not only possible but essential. No matter how fast things change, the principles of empathy, integrity, and transparency remain steadfast allies in the world of interpersonal communication.

Bridging the digital wall by tapping into the essence of human beings is the path to a healthier, more collaborative, and prosperous world.

About Dmitry

Nominated as HackerNoon Contributor of the Year in Data Security, Hacking, and Information Security and a member of the Forbes Technology Council, Dmitry Mishunin has taken the stage as a speaker at IT conferences around the world.

Dmitry is the founder and CEO of HashEx, a leading cybersecurity company specializing in Web3 and blockchain. He is a tech-savvy entrepreneur and has extensive experience working with global IT markets, ranging from start-ups to corporations. He possesses a deep knowledge of IT product development, and by leveraging a scientific approach to business, alongside the goal of creating a new economic landscape, Dmitry hopes to make a significant impact in modern technology fields and cybersecurity.

Dmitry is renowned for his expertise in cutting-edge technologies, scientific research on vulnerabilities in decentralized systems (DeFi), security audits, and the security of financial transactions in decentralized applications. He is actively involved in investing in tech start-ups, hedging against investment risks.

Dmitry continues to apply his education and experiential knowledge with his international blockchain security company, HashEx. Under Dmitry's management, HashEx has become a leader in the fields of cybersecurity and smart contracts auditing. Since its creation, the company has conducted over twelve hundred audits and helped preserve more than $3.4 billion worth of investor funds.

Dmitry holds a bachelor's degree in solid state physics and a master's degree in applied mathematics and physics, with expertise in modern materials and nanotechnologies. Dmitry also holds a master of business administration degree.

In his spare time you will find Dmitry snowboarding, kitesurfing, or track racing. He might also be enjoying the company of his preferred pets, cats, particularly red Maine coons.

You can connect with Dmitry:

- www.linkedin.com/in/dmitrymishunin
- https://hashex.org

CHAPTER 13

EMBRACING THE JOURNEY

Where True Impact Takes Root

By Andrew Brennan

"**H**e's passed," the somber voice on the other end said. Overwhelmed with sadness and disbelief, I had no idea how I would again grapple with the loss of someone so important in my life.

Without any thought, compassion, or mercy, cancer's grip had now claimed the lives of two of my closest friends and was rapidly degrading a third friend's.

I'm more contemplative these days with a greater awareness of not only my mortality but more so the significance and impact of others' lives on my own.

I find myself prioritizing the lasting impact that I might have on my children, my friends, my work colleagues, and even strangers.

So more so than ever, I strive to act with purpose, to add value to people's lives and model behavior that I hope provides a lasting impact on those around me.

You see, I am not a scientist or a clinician but rather a procurement leader, a patron of those who research, educate, train, and discover in schools, colleges, and universities across the country.

Most people have no idea what a procurement leader is or does. It's a job that goes largely unnoticed by most of the world but is vital to the success of every organization and our future.

My specific role is focused on helping educational institutions secure the services, supplies, and equipment they need to maintain their campuses, serve their students, and continue to teach and graduate the next generation of professionals, innovators, scientists, and clinicians who will change our world and hopefully save lives.

It is no secret that university operating budgets are shrinking. Compounding that issue, growing demands continue to be placed on those same institutions year after year, essentially being expected to do more with less.

In my current role, I lead a team of like-minded individuals whose primary responsibility is to create as much competition as possible among the suppliers who provide products and services to institutions. Not only are we focused on driving down the total cost of ownership, saving the institutions precious educational dollars, but we are also creating win-win partnerships.

At the time my closest friends passed away, I was working for the Louisiana State University Health Sciences Center. My experiences there helped me realize that although I am not the researcher or the scientist, my work was a lifeline for those who were. Every sourcing event, contract, purchase order mattered. Every discount I could get and timeline I could expedite was a small but valid contribution to the fight against cancer. The professionals working tirelessly to battle the disease could do their work only if they had the supplies and equipment they needed to do so!

I wonder how often people pause and take the time to think about all the layers of impact that surround their work. Most days it may seem as if you just push paper, or just send emails, or just create spreadsheets. But none of us "just" do anything.

Everyone plays a vital role in the bigger picture, and often we'll never have any idea how truly far-reaching our impact really is.

As I am sure you can imagine, I encounter significant resistance in my work. Pretty much daily.

The suppliers have sales targets to meet and aren't interested in lowering their pricing. The schools need supplies and equipment but need to spend less.

Essentially, my team sits as the liaison between corporations and educational institutions, doing our best to negotiate win-win scenarios, persuading organizations with totally competing agendas to collaborate for mutual benefit and success.

This truly is a challenge, but I wholeheartedly believe in the transformative power of education. After all, the generation of students being educated today are the ones who will be making a global impact tomorrow!

I see my role as a vital cog in a much bigger wheel.

If I am not successful in my role, the wheel has the potential to stop turning.

I've spent the past fifteen years navigating this challenging environment, and I've learned a few successful strategies when I need to exert influence. Surprisingly, these same strategies have come in very handy as a father of five as well.

Because it doesn't matter if you need to persuade one of your children to redefine success or persuade a multimillion-dollar corporation to adjust its pricing model, the basic principles of persuasion are the same, the first being an unwavering passion for the mission before you.

When I am faced with a negotiator who isn't interested in conceding on a particular point, rather than getting frustrated, I return to my passion for the mission.

I don't want to antagonize them. What I will do, which is much more aligned with who I am, is inspire them to shift their perspective by painting a vivid picture.

I help to show them how their concessions would reverberate beyond the walls of the schools and out into the world, ultimately contributing to the betterment of society. I share important research happening at universities, hoping that by illustrating the critical importance of that work, I can foster a sense of shared responsibility among us all.

I find that every time I take this approach, I am invigorated and reconnected to my purpose and the enthusiasm becomes contagious.

THE LOWEST COMMON DENOMINATOR

A few years back while at the LSU Health Sciences Center, I got a call from a research professor at the LSU Stanley S. Scott Cancer Center.

He had been tirelessly trying to procure new laptops for his team but was struggling with one of the suppliers. The supplier wasn't understanding the validity of this professor's request and wouldn't make any adjustments to the university's contractual specifications.

By the time the professor reached out to me, he was extremely frustrated and emotionally compromised. I decided to visit him in person.

Struggling to understand him in his emotional state and our language barrier, he and I weren't communicating well. I needed him to compose himself and explain his needs to me so that I could go back to the supplier and negotiate on his behalf. After about twenty minutes of getting yelled at without getting a word in, I reached for the pad of sticky notes on his desk, wrote the words "Cancer took my friends," and slid the pad to his side of the desk. He looked down at my note, halted his tirade, and said, "I'm sorry."

Over the next thirty minutes he explained his research to me in depth, emphasizing the importance of his team's work and the potential impact on cancer research. This wasn't some typical scheme for an exception to the university's standard laptop specifications. Securing laptops with these specific specifications would allow this professor's team to perform high-level computations much quicker, accelerating his research.

I asked a lot of questions. I wanted him to know that I was listening in a way that the supplier wasn't. As we finished, I committed to doing everything in my power to help get him what he needed. I took his research and its projected impact back to the supplier. I started with one simple question: "Have you been personally impacted by cancer?" It was immediately evident, by his facial expression, that the supplier representative had felt the same loss I had. From that point on, the conversation became about how the university and his company could collaborate to assist not only this professor but any of the other professors in the cancer center as well.

Why had I been successful where our professor wasn't?

I was successful because a powerful method of persuasion is connecting with others at the lowest common denominator: our humanity.

Regardless of our age, background, gender, or title, we all share the same basic human needs—to be listened to, to be understood, to know that we are not alone and that others empathize and share similar life struggles.

In any negotiation, listening and connecting at the most fundamental level fosters empathy and unity, fortifying the fact that despite our differences and unique challenges, we all have an innate desire to connect and make a difference.

MINDSET SHIFT AND REDEFINING SUCCESS

I live in an unpredictable and potentially volatile environment, knowing that at any moment the atmosphere could change from calm and peaceful to frantic and dramatic.

No, I don't live on the side of an active volcano, even though sometimes it feels like it! It's just life with two seventeen-year-old daughters.

If, like me, you have also parented teenagers, you understand all too well the daily tightrope act suspended over a sea of turbulence. It's a wild ride, rife with drama, suspense, action, and adventure.

I have made my share of mistakes, and through those mistakes I've learned that sometimes the best way to support my daughters isn't to dictate solutions to the problems they bring to my wife and me, but rather to ask questions guiding *them* to arrive at their own solution.

One of my daughters is the goalkeeper on her soccer team. Recently, she has been having a hard time. Though she's performing at the top of her game, her team repeatedly loses. During a recent game, she had played so well that the referee and even the opposing team's coaches applauded her performance. Yet when she got in the car, she broke down in tears. By now I have learned not to try and "fix" the situation. Instead, I focused on trying to influence her mindset by asking questions:

"Why did you come to the game today?"

"What are *you* personally trying to accomplish on the field?"

To which she replied, "I'm trying to play the best I can."

I asked her questions about specific saves where she had done everything right. I asked her to describe how she felt in those moments.

I wanted her to tune in to the fact that despite the global outcome, she was doing exactly what she set out to do, achieve her personal best. Essentially, I was helping her to redefine winning.

It worked!

She began to realize that true success is measured by more than the score at the end of the game.

Whenever I am trying to persuade someone to shift their mindset, a solid strategy I deploy is to ask pointed questions guiding them to redefine what success truly looks like.

Negotiators will *always* leave room on the table, and most are trained to concede very little or nothing at all. My team and I see it as our responsibility to ask questions that go beyond the initial objections and move to collaborate with the supplier to redefine success.

I ask questions such as:

"What are your short- and long-term goals with this university?"

"What is your most desirable outcome?"

"How would you define a successful relationship with this institution?"

People will typically respond that success looks like an immediate increase in sales across campus, but that's just the frontline response. I ask them how valuable a five-year contract would be over a three-year contract. I challenge them to shift their mindset and consider the lifetime value of a strategic partnership with a university rather than a short-term transactional one. Eventually, the supplier begins to embrace the vision and begins to shift their mindset from "winning" to true success.

HERE BE DRAGONS

"You meet in a tavern..." is the quintessential opening line for tabletop role-playing games.

I've had a lifelong passion for tabletop games, especially Dungeons and Dragons. I had no idea that my fantasy realm adventures would become foundational for navigating the real-world realm of business.

Dungeons and Dragons wasn't just about slaying monsters, casting spells, and collecting magical items; it was an immense open world for creative problem-solving, masterful negotiations, interpersonal relationship building, and most importantly role-playing. As a Dungeon Master, I learned the art of storytelling, navigating conflict, and to think from another person's perspective. I learned how to identify my resources and use them most effectively. I learned to think on my feet and anticipate the next moves, all skills that became invaluable tools in business.

Not long ago in a training sequence, I introduced a role-playing exercise to my team. I invited them to role-play with me and each other, immersing themselves in the motivations, fears, and desires that might cause a supplier to respond or behave in a certain way. It was surprisingly well received and tremendously effective! Though awkward and uncomfortable at first, it helped my team better understand *both* sides of the negotiation, strengthening their empathetic muscles.

They learned to come alongside their negotiation counterparts, meet them where they are, and help elevate their understanding. This is crucial in order to have any chance of getting them to your position. Seeing things from the other side's perspective illuminates the obstacles that are stifling collaboration and impeding a mutually beneficial solution.

Like magic, you begin to understand their motivations, fears, and desires. Wielding that magic, you can cast a spell targeted specifically at their objections, needs, pain points, and desired outcomes.

What was once a cacophony of voices clamoring for control is now a harmonious melody weaving together the fabric of collaboration and agreement.

Not only will the influence and impact be felt far and wide, but heroes will have been made, gleaming with pride and satisfaction for uniting adversarial kingdoms for mutual prosperity and collective growth.

Journey Before Destination

I try to live my life with the ideology behind the phrase "Journey Before Destination." Every day, I put on a silicone bracelet with those words written on it. And every morning when I slide it on and every evening when I slide it off again, I say those words aloud.

For me it means that wherever I am trying to go or end up in life is not as important as who I become or whom or what I have encountered along the way.

I wear it to remind myself of why I do what I do and how I want to behave and feel while I do it.

I wear it to remind myself of the lessons my parents taught me, to do the right things for the right reasons no matter the cost.

I wear it to remind myself that life is short and that there is richness and beauty in capturing every single moment and challenge along the way.

And I wear it to remind myself of the infinitesimal role I play in the universe. I understand now that my role has the potential to set off a ripple effect of innovation and impact for thousands of people whose names I will never know. As does yours!

I hope that when you consider the influence you want to have on others in your lifetime, you won't be intimidated but rather inspired by the fact that you, yes you, might just lead a discussion, or make a decision, or develop a solution, or role-play a character, that impacts lives for years to come.

About Andrew

Before Andrew Brennan is anything, he is a loving husband, an invested father, a supportive friend, and a grateful son. He would not be who he is today without the love, encouragement, and guidance that he has received throughout his life from those who have mattered most. Those who have believed in him in the past and those who continue to believe in him today. His family, his truest friends, his mentors, real or fictional, are the water to his roots, helping him mature, adapt, and grow more resilient as he navigates the winds of life. They are the wellspring for his sated joy and happiness, helping him practice mindfulness and be fully present in every moment that life provides.

Professionally, Andrew is the senior vice president of sourcing for E&I Cooperative Services. He leads teams that specialize in strategic sourcing, contracting, procurement operations, and analytics, managing more than three billion dollars in annual spend, for more than six thousand higher-education and K-12 institutions across the United States.

Previously, Andrew worked as the assistant procurement director for the Louisiana State University Main Campus and Health Sciences Center. Geaux Tigers!

He graduated from Ferris State University with a degree in business and a specialization in professional golf management. Go Bulldogs!

Andrew is a change agent. His passion is for driving procurement transformation and excellence in both the public and private education sectors. He speaks at numerous education and procurement conferences to audiences across the US on the topics of sourcing best practice, procurement transformation, team development, and spend analytics.

Personally, he likes to explore the hidden depths of epic fantasy and science fiction; he game-masters tabletop role-playing games and enjoys bringing to life and giving voice to fictional characters; he rejuvenates by adventuring through the forests and mountains of the Appalachia; he enthusiastically cheers on the LSU Tigers with his beautiful wife, Tatiana, and their five kids, Peyton, Micah, Adrianna, Jackson, and Brianna; and he gets covered in mud wrestling with his five German shepherd dogs, Grace, Artemis, Nala, Raelyn, and Little Bear (LB).

Connect with Andrew: www.andrewjbrennan.com.

CHAPTER 14

INFLUENCING WITH INTEGRITY

Mastering the Art of Ethical Persuasion

By Zak Green

I pulled my phone from my pocket for probably the hundredth time that day, my heart quickening with anticipation as I tapped the little envelope icon to open my email.

Nothing.

Still nothing.

My inbox had become the most suspenseful box office thriller of the decade, and I was the anxious protagonist waiting for the storyline to deliver. The bosses were breathing down my neck, and as the minutes ticked away, the pressure was practically unbearable.

At the time, I was the global head of liquidity sales for AllianceBernstein (AB), and securing Cisco, a global technology giant renowned for cutting-edge networking solutions, would be a triumph. AB had all but exited the business in 2005. After interviewing with twenty executives, including CEO Seth Bernstein, in 2018 I made the case for them bringing me on board to lead this languishing legacy business. Now it was time to make good on my ambitious forecasts.

That night, feeling deflated and already rehearsing my "We gave it our best shot; we'll get them next time" speech to the leadership team, I decided to check one last time. I clicked open my email, and there it was. "Zak, thank you for your patience. We have approved AllianceBernstein. We look forward to working with you."

In the grand scheme of things, it was just an email, but in that moment, it was a giant sigh of relief and the culmination of months of hard work and back-and-forth.

Today, I'm a persuasion consultant.

As a native of New York City, I was born into a creative lineage, with an artist mother, a clothing manufacturer father, and a psychoanalyst stepfather. My upbringing was a kaleidoscope of influences. After attending Cornell University, I embarked on what you might call a diverse professional journey. As a self-described "late bloomer," my early career comprised roles as a paralegal for a prestigious law firm and a marketing associate for a major record label.

A pivotal turn in my career came when my friend Marc facilitated my entry into Wall Street and a position with the (then) prestigious firm Lehman Brothers. Navigating this world exposed me to a variety of personalities and provided invaluable lessons. Paying my early dues and mastering the art of business interactions propelled me through the ranks, resulting in over two decades of global sales leadership across three multinational firms.

During my most recent tenure with AB, I was able to help facilitate the *quadrupling* of the long dormant business in less than five years, without hiring a single salesperson. Throughout my career I've served a wide range of clients, including endowments, foundations, municipalities, sovereign wealth funds, and over 40 percent of Fortune 500 Companies™, ultimately raising over $150 billion in assets.

I share that because it seems an unlikely path for a guy who kicked off his adult life with a lack of direction and an obsession with classic rock!

I realize now that whatever success I've enjoyed can be attributed to a quality I have always leaned in to, and it's one I believe *anyone* can use to gain forward momentum: *curiosity.*

My insatiable curiosity about people *and their motivations* has been a constant thread in my life and has led to extraordinary relationships with highly influential people and many once-in-a-lifetime experiences.

When I think back to my early career with one particular grass-roots, family-owned asset management firm, it amazes me what we were able to accomplish from a makeshift office without any bells and whistles.

Here we were, a virtually unknown company competing with the giants of our industry such as Fidelity, BlackRock, and J.P. Morgan, hoping that our determination would be enough to draw attention away from the fact that almost no one had ever heard of us. Our success was completely dependent upon our ability to persuade our prospects to trust us and take a chance.

Have you ever been in a situation where you had no leg to stand on other than passion for your mission?

There's a science to it. Over the years, after successfully closing hundreds of business deals, I started to study the patterns of influence that had been most effective for me. I developed a kind of formula that I have used myself to raise more than $150 billion in capital, and I've taught it to hundreds of business leaders over the years.

It's not some sales system.

It's not software.

It's a way of engaging with the world that is rooted in the science of human behavior, and if you learn how to do it correctly, you can have the best chance of success.

I call it the Persuasion Path, and I now teach this method to teams and organizations all over the country.

Whether you're persuading someone to invest in your company, rallying a team behind a new initiative, or trying to win an argument with your spouse, persuasion works. No, not every argument, and not every time. And yes, sometimes you're probably still better off saying, "Honey you're right," but in most cases, persuasive communication is a powerful and strategic partner across all avenues of conversation.

The cornerstone of the Persuasion Path is building rapport and making a connection. This is because it's easier to influence and ultimately lead someone who views you as one of their own. I will teach you *how* to be like-minded with the audience you hope to persuade even when it appears there are no common objectives to be found.

While of course, nothing is a panacea, the following principles of the Persuasion Path are tools of influence and impact that have rarely let me down, and if you follow their lead, I can confidently predict a successful outcome for you too.

Do Your Emotional Homework

Emotional homework starts with gathering psychological insights about the individual(s) whom you're seeking to influence *before you get them in the room.* The more you know about how they operate, their hopes, fears, and pain thresholds, the better you'll be able to navigate the process and ultimately lead them.

This is not about simply googling the person, reviewing their LinkedIn profile, and calling it a day. This is about researching who they are as *people*—how they engage with the world, how they speak, what words they choose, and their body language. People like to be understood. Your task is to find and use information that will help you understand them.

When I first began my career, I was a no-name in the industry and had very little leverage. What I did have was guts and a feeling that no one was out of my league. I never shied away from speaking with someone more senior and wasn't intimidated by titles. At one point I downloaded a copy of the Fortune 500 List™, crafted something of a script in my head, and started cold-calling the CFOs of each of these companies, starting with then number one ExxonMobil, which became my first client.

I developed a consultative approach in which I wasn't calling looking for investment but rather for *knowledge*. I figured that everyone likes to demonstrate their knowledge. I would ask a question with genuine curiosity, and that would open the door for me to then propose my firm's differentiated offerings.

It was a reciprocal dance that proved to be very effective in building rapport and relationships, which are a coveted currency in the world of business negotiations.

Fast-forward a few years, and I had the opportunity to practice emotional homework again, this time in a very unique set of circumstances. The year was 2006, and at that point, while I had enjoyed quite a bit of success domestically with Fortune 500 Companies™ and many of the largest hedge funds in the country, I was particularly excited about a relationship I had begun to cultivate with the Bank of China.

To land a deal with that organization would be a doorway for our firm to move into a worldwide leadership role. I felt a lot of pressure to lead our company to the global stage. I wanted this for my team, for the firm, and for my own career ambitions. The stakes were high, and as the meeting date approached, I was almost embarrassed by our modest office. I imagined that these Chinese executives were used to being courted through fancy high-rise offices with sweeping views, shiny floors, and gigantic impressive lobbies. We didn't have any of that. We would be meeting them in a dark and windowless conference room, and that meant we'd have to work extra hard to capture and keep their attention.

Before the big day, I did my emotional homework.

In my pursuit of understanding cross-cultural dynamics, I discovered Geert Hofstede's cultural dimensions theory, particularly focusing on his Power Distance Index (PDI). His theory illuminated how different societies handle inequality and hierarchical structures, and *to what degree they revere those in positions of perceived authority.*

I learned that China has a high PDI ranking, which means they have a high reverence for authority. I also knew enough about the culture to be aware of the importance of ceremony. I realized then that meeting our highest-level executive would likely make a positive impression on the Bank of China team. If I could lean in to their regard for hierarchy and ceremony, I could perhaps draw their attention away from our cracked paint and dated digs and show our firm as both like-minded and differentiated.

I enlisted our chairman, an occasionally charming white-haired man in his seventies, to personally attend the meeting. I asked that he show five to ten minutes after the meeting began to have the greatest impact on our guests. I further asked that he deliver gifts in alignment with my research. My "emotional home-work" laid forth a path that I hoped would be a differentiated one, and one where I felt our strategy would have a high likelihood of moving the needle and *quickly*.

The approach proved successful and secured our first interna-tional client. This experience not only marked a pivotal achieve-ment but also laid the foundation for my ongoing respect and reverence of the science *behind* persuasion.

Another element of emotional homework is to tune in to the universal truth that the things we think about the most will *irra-tionally* rise in importance in our minds.

Again, armed with this knowledge, how then can we best ensure our clients continue to think about us and the solutions we are proposing? One way might be to reach out to them with consistency but always with constructive, relevant, and differen-tiated information specific to *their* business or needs. Maybe you just read they had a particularly strong quarter or saw news of a potential acquisition. Anything you can do to reach out to them *plausibly* with information that's meant to help *them* is a step in the right direction.

Lastly, play to the inner child in all of us that still loves receiving gifts. Reciprocity is a cornerstone of persuasion because people are hardwired to reciprocate favors. If you'd like someone to do some-thing for you tomorrow, do something for them *today*. Better still, do something for them *yesterday*.

This might be sharing insights of a new risk they may have exposure to, taking them to dinner, or sending them a condolence card after the passing of a loved one. In other words, something that demonstrates that they are important to you. Ideally, your act should also display *empathy*, putting yourself in their shoes.

UNDERSTAND THAT SIMPLE EXPLANATIONS APPEAR MORE CREDIBLE THAN COMPLEX ONES

The philosophy of Occam's razor states that the simplest explanation is generally correct. This persuasion tip is rooted in that philosophy. It's important to understand that simplicity makes your ideas easy to understand, easy to remember, and easy to spread. Now of course we don't always have the luxury of providing an easy, simple solution, but we should strive to simplify our explanations to the extent possible and avoid wordy explanations that can be difficult to follow/absorb/believe.

Anyone who's put together a pitch deck or a PowerPoint knows that if your page is too wordy or has more than a few bullet points, you begin to lose your reader or your audience.

Here's an example: In my presentations I often draw from the O. J. Simpson trial. Roughly thirty years after the trial, what most people remember (other than the verdict) is "If it doesn't fit, you must acquit." Terse and memorable. It cut to the crux of the defense's strategy and was a call to action to the jury. The fact that it rhymed made it play in the jury's head like a familiar song.

PEOPLE ARE MORE INFLUENCED BY THE DIRECTION OF THINGS THAN THE CURRENT STATE

Another principle of the Persuasion Path might drag you out of your comfort zone, but the ROI is worth it. It starts with an understanding that people are more influenced by the *direction* of things than the current state of things.

For example, if I know going into a meeting that my client is unhappy with the current state of things, I'll open the meeting with that fact, immediately sharing that their poorly performing portfolio is now improving, thanks to some of the specific steps we've taken to address it. Acknowledging less than stellar results can be effective in building trust with clients. The client will see you as a sincere and confident expert rather than an incompetent dodger of difficult conversations. Tackling the tough stuff head-on allows you to capture the high ground and positions you as the adult in the room.

Further, if you can guess what people are thinking—at the very moment they think it—and call it out even if it's an uncomfortable truth, the subject bonds with you for being like-minded.

It might sound something like, "Hi, Steve. I know what you're thinking—our performance has been lackluster recently. You're right. Here's why, and more importantly, these are the steps we've taken to address it and address it quickly." The takeaway here is that Steve sees that his feelings are both acknowledged and addressed head-on. You own up to it and state decisive actions being taken to address it quickly. The issue is now in the rearview mirror.

A Few Closing Thoughts

"If you don't pay appropriate attention to what has your attention, it will take more of your attention than it deserves."

Those words were written by author and productivity consultant David Allen, and they echo the principles of the Persuasion Path.

If you stay present, become self-aware, and pay respectful attention, not only can you avoid the embarrassment of missing important details, but you can serve and lead in a more powerful way.

Attention is one of the sincerest forms of respect. Where there's respect, there's collaboration.

Collaboration is forging an even energy exchange with people you actively seek to know and respect.

It's also the true key to lasting influence and far-reaching impact.

About Zak

People would ask, "Wait, *how* did you get into the Monaco Yacht Club during the Monaco Grand Prix?" I'd say, "I asked with the right intonation."

Zachary "Zak" Green was born and raised in New York City. He is the son of an artist mother, a clothing manufacturer father, and a psychoanalyst stepfather.

He graduated from Cornell University, where he studied economics and psychology. A self-described "late bloomer," after graduating, his early jobs included working as a paralegal for a prominent law firm and a marketing associate for a large record label. At night he would indulge in his classic rock music addiction and play the drums to some of his favorite drummers.

A few years after college a friend helped him land a job at Lehman Brothers. His role at Lehman gave him an early taste of Wall Street. The role gave him exposure to a demanding, fast-paced new world and early lessons in navigating some, ahem, challenging personalities. It was some of the best schooling he could have received.

Paying his early dues and *paying attention to people and their motivations* led to several promotions that culminated in more than two decades of global sales leadership across three multi-national firms. He most recently served as global head of liquidity sales for AllianceBernstein, where he roughly quadrupled that business in less than five years with *zero headcount*. He's counted endowments, municipalities, Sovereign Wealth Funds, and more than 40 percent of Fortune 500 Companies™ as clients and has raised over $150 billion in assets throughout his career.

An endless curiosity about people, how to read and motivate them, has been one constant throughout Zak's life. He's been a student and teacher of influence and persuasion, the science behind it, and has crafted a Master Class that has become a cornerstone for business leaders seeking to enhance or optimize their persuasion skills. His role as a *persuasion consultant* has allowed him to mentor and address influence-based challenges for organizations all over the world.

Away from his "day jobs" Zak is also an early fintech inventor, holding patents for compliance-based trading protocols focused on leveling the playing field. His "Systems and Methods for Controlling Portfolios" (patent numbers 8,095,446 and 8,660,928) aims to democratize investing by revolutionizing how investors safeguard and rebalance the $50T+ across Fund/ETF investments.

Zak resides in NYC and Southampton with his wife and their two children.

Connect with Zak on LinkedIn at www.linkedin.com/in/zgreen.

CHAPTER 15

TIME TRAVEL COULD BE YOUR BIGGEST COMPETITIVE EDGE

By Vaun Podlogar

We're not going to make it.

We're not going to make it, and it will be my fault.

A large banner across the storefront announced that the new well-known, big-box retailer would finally open its doors in just two weeks. The residents of the upscale coastal community in Florida had been patiently watching the construction, and now they wanted to see inside the beautiful new building.

Local media had been advertising for weeks, and the grand opening had become a daily topic of local conversations.

Confidence was in the air, everyone assuming that in ten days we would cut the ribbon, open the doors, and celebrate another successful launch.

But on my end it wasn't looking good.

I was still dealing with tech gremlins sabotaging the very software we needed to finish my portion of the job. I felt the weight from the expectations of the Wall Street investors bearing down on me.

I couldn't escape the thought that the fate of an entire operation rested on my ability to navigate the bureaucratic labyrinth before time ran out.

Sixteen trucks filled with merchandise idled in a hot parking lot, serving as a visual reminder of what was at stake. I understood the impending chaos that would occur if I failed to deliver, both for this project and the potential damage to my company's reputation. Failure wasn't an option.

With less than two weeks until the grand opening, I picked up the phone and spoke to a random IT guy, who zeroed in on the problem and solved it! After just that one phone call, it all fell mercifully into place, and the store opened on time.

You see, I'm the owner of State Permits Inc. at www.permit. com, and our business is to manage and expedite the construction permit process, perform code searches, and champion sign authorizations. Our company has had the privilege of working with some of the biggest brands in the world. If a Nike store or Starbucks opens in your neighborhood, there's a good chance I had something to do with it. When I first joined this business, there was no such thing as email, no AI software, no zoom meetings. I had two tools at my disposal to succeed: my landline phone and an unwavering commitment to fulfilling my purpose.

At this point, you might be thinking, "Is this guy saying that his purpose in life is in permits and applications? Boring!"

While on the surface, approvals and permits may sound like mundane paperwork, they play a vital role in sustaining a town's vibrant energy. When a corporation opens a new business, it breathes life into the local economy, generates jobs, and creates a positive ripple effect that impacts the entire community.

And it's a lot harder than it sounds!

Hundreds of lives would have been affected and millions of dollars stalled had I not been able to pull through for the store in Florida.

Every day is a delicate dance with the municipal gatekeepers who often are more trained in constructing roadblocks than facilitating progress. Every day, I am met with resistance. So, my job isn't just about acquiring permits; it's about convincing reluctant custodians of approvals that cooperation is not only essential but beneficial for everyone involved.

That's where the art of persuasion becomes my ally.

A substantial portion of my day is spent cultivating a sense of shared purpose, transforming what may feel like an obligatory duty into an enthusiastic collaboration. It's not just about securing permits; it's about ensuring that each stakeholder recognizes the value of their contribution and executes their responsibilities with a sense of pride and purpose.

It's not easy to hold the attention of one of the busiest individuals in the city and convince them that your project is more important than everyone else's.

Yet nine times out of ten, I get what I need. I do it with what I call Empathetic Persuasion.

Why Time Travel Is Your Ticket to Success

Empathetic Persuasion is a technique I've used to get very important people on the phone, accomplish seemingly impossible goals, and generate millions of dollars in business.

Anyone can use it.

All it requires is your ability to time-travel. Stay with me.

We live in a high-tech, low-connection society driven by self-promotion and technological advancements. The machines, data, robots, and software designed to make our lives easier often make things more complicated.

The allure of screens and virtual interactions overshadows the depth of face-to-face communication and genuine human experiences. In the quest for efficiency, our dependence on technology can distance us from the empathy that defines our *humanity*.

Long before the internet, companies such as Sears and Ford made billions by leveraging resources that are ignored today— their brains, hearts, and genuine interest in solving problems, helping people, and making a positive impact on the world.

People may love technology. They may geek out over the fact that they can create Facebook ads that might reach someone across the globe, who then *might* complete a contact form and *might* take the action you want them to take.

But that's a lot of "mights," and this uncertainty creates distance between you and your target audience. Let's remember what happened in 2020.

The lockdown that came with the pandemic reminded us of the importance of human connection. When the ability to be with other people was taken from us, it hit hard!

In fact, there was a massive decline in mental health that was largely attributed to the lack of human interaction.

So, while it's tempting to be wowed and distracted by all the technological bells and whistles at our disposal today, you can edge out the competition by remembering this:

Business—*good* business—is *personal.*

You want to stand out today?

Time-travel back to a pre-internet era and go back to basics. Have actual conversations. Try to connect. And listen when someone is talking!

"You're two thousand cold calls away from being a millionaire."

Those were the words of Dan Pena, the businessman known as the Trillion Dollar Man who boasts a $500 million net worth.

I don't know about you, but I'll take advice from a guy worth $500 million.

I wouldn't be nearly as successful as I am today if I was afraid to pick up the phone and call a stranger. Granted, back when I started, that was my only option.

Yet even as email, Zoom, online chats, and other tools became available, the phone remained my ride-or-die wingman. However, Gen Z seems almost afraid of the telephone.

There are countless memes circulating the internet that poke fun at this terror of talking to a live human being. Things such as: "I'm sorry I didn't answer my phone when you called. I don't use it for that." "Sorry I missed your call. I was staring at the phone in horror, wondering why you called instead of just texting."

I'm not sure what everyone is afraid of, but I know that if I shared that aversion to picking up the phone, I wouldn't be nearly as successful as I am today.

A while back I was working on a project for a store opening in a mall in Sacramento...on Black Friday!

Brick-and-mortar stores generate *billions* of dollars on Black Friday.

Most businesses are operating at a loss throughout the year.

But then, like magic, Black Friday swoops in and turns the tables. That's the day when they go from being in the red to finally making some green, and suddenly, it's like the whole year was just a warm-up for the main event. It's the time when businesses can finally take a breather and say, "We made it!"

As you can imagine, a grand opening on Black Friday was a highly anticipated event that the company was counting on for a major boost in sales.

They needed help getting permits approved and were hitting roadblocks. They came to me with just four days until the deadline.

On the Monday before Black Friday, I started making calls. I called the reviewers. I called their bosses. I called every five minutes until I reached whom I needed to reach. I explained the economic impact this store opening could have on their community, and I used empathetic persuasion to get them excited about their role in it.

By Tuesday we had our permit. The general contractor worked through Thanksgiving, and with quite a bit of fanfare the store opened on Black Friday.

The next Monday, that client called to share that they had done more than $180,000 per day in sales over that one weekend. That was back in the 1990s, so that's equivalent to more than $1,000,000 today. They were so grateful that we had helped them achieve their goal.

All I did was pick up the phone!

Of course, I use email a lot today too, but the nuances conveyed through tone, inflection, and real-time dialogue create a level of understanding and connection that text-based interactions cannot replicate. Not only does a phone call foster quicker decision-making and conflict resolution, but it also adds the personal touch needed to build lasting relationships.

I'm not suggesting we throw out our computers and go back to pioneer living. Imagine, however, being in a time-sensitive situation and sending an email to solve it. You have to assume that the recipient will look at it. You have no idea if they opened it. And instead of calling to find out, what do most people do? Send a follow-up email.

By that time a deadline is missed, and your reputation is in the toilet!

I've created more impact than I ever thought possible by doing what most other people are unwilling to do—picking up the phone!

"You can make more friends in two months by becoming interested in other people than you can in two years by trying to get other people interested in you."

That's a passage from the classic book *How to Win Friends and Influence People* by Dale Carnegie.

The second part of Empathetic Persuasion is to be genuinely interested in other people.

In the age of relentless self-promotion, "look-at-me" culture, true interest in other people is a breath of fresh air. Let's look back to a time when success wasn't measured by likes and hashtags but by a genuine commitment to others.

Decades ago businesses thrived by being genuinely interested in people, understanding their problems, and actively working to solve them. Back then, innovation wasn't about your number of social media followers; it was a driving force for advancement.

If you're a business owner, it doesn't matter what your niche is—you're in the business of solving problems and helping people. I can't think of any industry that isn't built on those two concepts.

To be successful, you've got to be willing to put your own immediate goal aside and instead, tune in to what would serve the person on the other end of the phone line.

My goal is always to get the permit approved on time and within budget. However, if I go into a conversation laser-focused on my own intentions, I won't get very far. The people I talk to are trained to resist. "No" is their default response.

I must instead be genuinely curious about how what I want is beneficial to *them*.

There is a passage from Dale Carnegie's book in which he writes, "Personally I am very fond of strawberries and cream, but I have found that for some strange reason, fish prefer worms. So when I went fishing, I didn't think about what I wanted. I thought about what they wanted. I didn't bait the hook with strawberries and cream. Rather, I dangled a worm or grasshopper in front of the fish and said: 'Wouldn't you like to have that?'

"Why not use the same common sense when fishing for people?"

It makes sense, right?

It reminds me of the conventional "wisdom" that tells us to treat others how we want to be treated. I encourage you to treat others how *they* want to be treated. What's important to them might be different from what's important to you. You won't know unless you're willing to be curious.

You may be against a deadline. You may have a very clear, straightforward goal you need to accomplish.

Forget about it.

During your conversation (which you're now having by phone), forget your end goal and remember that you're talking to a human.

Humans need to feel good. They need to feel heard and understood. They want to know that the time they spend with you will result in some kind of win for them.

Figure out how you can help them win, and you'll get your yes.

Easy buttons are the fast food of life—satisfying now, regrettable later.

Corners are sharp! If you cut them, they cut *you*.

Most of the time the people you're working with can tell if you're taking a shortcut and can smell laziness a mile away. Every time you push the easy button and take a shortcut, your character takes a hit.

If there's one thing I've noticed over decades of leading teams and navigating the business world, it's this: How you do one thing is how you do everything.

It's true for all of us. If you take shortcuts in a business project, you probably try to take them at home too.

If you avoid tough conversations with a prospect or colleague, you probably avoid the same kinds of conversations with your loved ones.

Be diligent in your commitment to doing what you say you're going to do, following through, and acting with integrity even if it takes a little longer and a little more work.

Persuasion isn't always about the words you use but the behaviors you exhibit. Treating every interaction with respect is sometimes more powerfully persuasive than a list of data to back your argument!

Be the kind of person you would want to do business with.

Don't Forget the Icing

The Florida store opening that almost didn't happen will live in my memory as one of the most stressful weeks of my life. Of course, I was relieved it all worked out, but I didn't crack open some champagne and relax.

That's because you've got to remember the icing on the cake.

When it was all said and done, I made sure to send a handwritten thank-you note to the permit office. I shared how their decision positively impacted the entire community and reminded them of what was made possible by their cooperation.

Part of exercising persuasion is remembering that empathy is not a one-time thing.

To truly stand out and be successful, you've got to remain curious and make human connections a top priority. That's how you become memorable. That's how you become profitable.

Most importantly, that's how you build your reputation as the person who always gets the job done.

About Vaun

Vaun Podlogar's journey in the realm of commercial construction began during the early 1990s, when he found himself immersed in the intricacies of permit acquisition while working within the permit division of a national general contractor, State Construction. It was here that Vaun gained invaluable firsthand experience navigating bureaucratic hurdles and recognizing the critical need for a more efficient approach to the permitting process.

In 1994 a pivotal moment arose with the restructuring of State Construction, leading to the creation of a separate entity dedicated solely to permits: State Permits Inc. This transition provided Vaun with the opportunity to materialize his vision of revolutionizing industry practices. His ability to innovate swiftly established him as a trusted ally for clients seeking customized permit solutions.

Under Vaun's astute leadership, State Permits has evolved into a cornerstone of the market, renowned for its exceptional management of commercial permit processes. Specializing in a wide array of services including commercial and retail remodels, rollouts, multisite programs, signage due diligence, solar permits, licensing, and more, SPI has expanded its reach from its humble beginnings in Wisconsin to serving clients across North America.

Vaun's unwavering dedication to delivering unparalleled service isn't merely a motto; it's a fundamental principle woven into the fabric of his company's culture. He cultivates an environment where client satisfaction reigns supreme, viewing each interaction as an opportunity to forge enduring relationships built on trust and reliability.

With over three decades of experience overseeing thousands of projects across various municipalities, Vaun has become a sought-after business and life coach, as well as a dynamic speaker for seminars, keynotes, workshops, and other professional engagements. Leveraging his expertise, he addresses a spectrum of topics including time management, remote work strategies, email efficiency, and optimizing systems and procedures.

Vaun's influence and expertise have left an indelible mark on esteemed companies such as Starbucks, CVS, Famous Footwear, Sterling Jewelers, and Party City, among many others. His infectious enthusiasm for life is a testament to his belief that every moment is an adventure to be savored.

To learn more about Vaun Podlogar and State Permits Inc., visit www.vaun.com and www.permit.com.

CHAPTER 16

POKER, PROBABILITIES, AND PROFIT FROM CHINATOWN TO WALL STREET

Six Principles for Winning at Life!

By Ron Mark

A s I stepped through the doorway of my friend's lavish home, I was awestruck.

We were in Lincoln Park, the wealthy side of Chicago, and a world away from the tiny apartment I shared with my parents and three older brothers.

The foyer, framed by the kind of butterfly staircase I had only seen in movies, was bigger than my entire home, and the sunlight streamed through the window, highlighting the shine of the polished wood.

In that moment, surrounded by such splendor, something within me shifted. The realization that there was another way to live suddenly hit me, and inside, a new determination came to life. "What does your dad do?" I asked. "I don't know," my friend replied nonchalantly. "I think he's a trader."

I envisioned my future shining with promise and framed in luxury and made up my mind in that moment that whatever his father did, I would do too.

My parents were born in Hong Kong and came to America with nothing but courage and a fierce determination to forge a good life for me and my brothers. They opened a modest Chop Suey restaurant. Every penny they made went to putting us kids through school. My earliest memories are of working long hours in that restaurant and watching them toil away night after night, cooking, cleaning tables, and doing their best to hold it all together.

I'm so grateful for how hard my parents worked to provide for us, but after that day in Lincoln Park, the thought of spending my entire life in Chop Suey jail seemed unbearable. I went to the library and checked out every book they had on financial management and trading.

As soon as I was out of school, I went to the Chicago Board of Trade eager to start making my millions. We have two major exchanges in Chicago. The problem was that it was a closed-door network back then. If you weren't born into it or invited, you wouldn't get in. I tried to get my resume into the hands of the right people but was repeatedly rejected.

It was disheartening, but I wasn't giving up. I wanted that butterfly staircase.

One day while I was working in the restaurant, a customer came in and sat down in my section. He was wearing a trading jacket, so I took my chance to ask some questions. I told him about my dream and asked if he'd let me know of any opportunity to work in the exchange.

One day he came in and handed me a phone number for a guy named Tom Price. Tom had just opened his trading firm. I called him up and quite transparently said, "Sir, I don't know anything. I'd like to come and learn. I'll come and work for free for six months, and if I haven't proved myself valuable to you after that, you can tell me to go."

He hired me. I was ecstatic. I thought I was joining a huge firm, but when I walked in, the only people working were Tom and his wife, and my "office" was a folding chair in the corner.

That was thirty years ago. That firm grew exponentially over the years, and today, as I write this, I'm in the process of buying it.

I've enjoyed a long and successful career as a financial adviser and money manager, and what I've discovered over the years is that the principles of financial management, martial arts, and poker parallel the fundamental principles necessary for achieving any goal in life.

HERE ARE SIX PRINCIPLES TO LIVE BY

1. Compound the little things.

I was a tiny kid. In middle school I peaked at 120 pounds and five-foot-two. Not only was I small and skinny, but I found myself in the tough transition from a primarily Chinese grade school to a school in which I was a minority. Like a lot of new kids, I was bullied. I started studying martial arts and became obsessed with being the best I could be. I trained ten hours a day when I could and ran ten miles most days, and by the time I was a junior in high school, I was a solid 155 pounds and no one was messing with me. I was training mixed martial arts before it was even called MMA.

I knew then that whatever I set my mind to I could achieve if I worked hard and followed the right steps in the right order.

I had to practice and train. I had to change my diet and amend how I spent my free time. But I was willing to do whatever it took, *until* it took.

If I had tried to be a master of martial arts at 120 pounds with no confidence, I would have failed. I had to take it one benchmark at a time.

All benefits in life come from compound interest. Start becoming exceptional at *one thing*. Consistency lies at the heart of true success.

Think about your goals and what you can do every day to get there. Then, break that task down to an absurdly small level. Stay at that level for weeks, a month, or more—whatever it takes for you to get bored with it. After that, take it up a notch very slowly, raising the bar by no more than 10 percent.

The point is to make the tasks you're doing so minor that it seems as though it's not worth doing. That keeps the stakes low and makes the task a no-brainer day to day.

Imagine you want to save money but don't have much to start with. Put one dollar in your savings account every day. If you start saving one dollar a day in month one, raising that by ten cents a month for one year, you could save $435 by the end of the year.

It's a start.

The tiptoeing here isn't just about the money you save. It's also about the habit you're creating. As you stick to it, you begin to feel pride in your discipline.

Sometimes it's intimidating to have a goal of making a big impact. So, choose to make smaller impacts, but again and again until one day you realize that a big impact has indeed been made. This is why Einstein said compound interest is the eighth wonder of the world.

2. Automate.

When it comes to saving money, you could use technology such as automatic transfers to automate your daily actions. I teach my children to save and invest 60 percent of their after-tax income. Set it up so that 60 percent gets automatically moved to another bank account where you have no debit card and limited access.

It could also mean using spending trackers to simplify money management. Again, the point is to make those small, day-to-day tasks as simple as possible.

But what if the goal is something different? Maybe your goal is to land a new client who's been resisting an appointment with you.

Schedule a follow-up email to go out every week for a month or two.

Automation is the key to consistency, and consistency is hard to ignore!

Eventually, either because they finally notice you or because they want to shut you up, you'll get the face time you need to seal the deal.

3. Reverse-engineer success.

In my second year at the exchange, I was a victim of a scam. A person opened an account and deposited a foreign check for $1,000,000. It turned out that the check was fake! He ended up losing $300,000 before we figured out that his check bounced. As his broker I was responsible for the loss if the client didn't pay, and this guy wasn't paying. I was twenty-two years old, had no money, and was now in $300,000 worth of debt. I was devastated.

I reverse-engineered what I had to do. I knew that to make enough money to pay that debt off in sixty months, I would need to make an additional $5,000 a month. How the hell was I going to do *that*?

I would do it by making it a singular focus. I started having more meetings with potential clients and learned to supercharge my relationships. I worked overtime. I spent days on end looking for new clients and would end each day completely exhausted. But I paid off every cent.

I was able to do what at first seemed impossible because my early martial arts training had taught me the importance of habits.

If I told you that you could dramatically change your life, increase your happiness and attract wealth, but you had to spend fifteen minutes a day on a new habit, would you do it?

The truth is, change doesn't require long stretches of sacrifice; it requires short commitments practiced consistently over time.

There are a lot of people out there saying they want to change their lives, yet visit them a year later, and they are in the exact same place, with the same challenges, same body, same routines, and same questions that seem to never get answered.

And I get it!

After all, changing your life feels like a pretty big undertaking. It's enough to scare anyone into staying the same. Remember, everything you will ever want is on the other side of fear.

The key is to pair your new small daily tasks with anything that's already part of your routine. Piggyback off what exists. That connection can make it easier to fold new tasks into your daily rituals so they become second nature.

For example, maybe schedule your small daily money habits around your morning routine. If you're waiting for coffee to brew in the morning, use that as your time to check your savings, spending, and retirement apps.

Piggybacking off existing routines is a simple but powerful way to infuse your life with new habits that cultivate the conditions for change to take place.

Small habits lead to BIG impact!

4. Look for mentors.

"I'm pregnant."

I'll never forget the shock of hearing my wife utter those words. We got married at the age of twenty-three, I had less than two hundred dollars in my bank account, and now a baby was on the way!

I went into total panic and knew that my plan for growth would have to go from baby steps to lightning speed. I needed to learn and fast. I reached out to people who were more knowledgeable than me and asked questions. I read books and took courses. These days you have YouTube, Google, Amazon Books, Audible, podcasts, and more. You have ten times the knowledge available and for free!

Back then I hunkered down and researched everything I could about the history of the market and what skills defined a good market technician. I got very comfortable learning to present and sell, and within five years, by which time we had had a second child, I could sit at a table with the most experienced market technicians in the world and hold my own.

When the stakes are high, knowledge is your greatest asset.

I was a poor Chinese kid from Chinatown. I didn't have a refined vocabulary, and sales didn't come naturally to me. I committed to learning everything I could to position myself as an authority in the room.

If you're heading into the arena, be it the board room or the negotiating table, start your preparation early. Do your research! The three Ps: Know the people, the product, and the process.

Every day, set aside five minutes to learn something new. For my clients who are just starting to save money, I encourage them to spend five minutes a day reading or watching financial news.

The point is to immerse yourself in the goal, and little by little, build a storehouse of knowledge you can pull from anytime to give you the edge you need.

5. Think in probabilities.

I could feel myself starting to sweat.

I sat at the green-felted table, the dim casino lights flickering overhead, and felt a rush of anticipation. I had the "nuts," and I had them trapped.

My journey into poker stemmed from my father's struggles with gambling and the inevitable strain it put on our family.

As I got older, I started to wonder why he always lost.

So I did what I had always done when I was feeling challenged. I researched. I learned that the casinos held an inherent advantage but that it was indeed possible to tip the odds in one's own favor. With practice I honed my ability to place the odds in my favor, or better yet, *wait* for the odds in your favor—an experience that later proved beneficial in my trading career. I eventually realized that winning in poker wasn't foolproof, but the experience taught me an invaluable lesson of thinking in probabilities.

Thinking in probabilities trains us to approach situations knowing there could be any number of outcomes. When you go into any business interaction with the understanding that nothing is certain, thinking in probabilities allows you to consider every possible angle and prepare for each.

Nothing is black and white, and the very nature of the market, and of life, is that it changes. When you make a decision, you cannot guarantee a good outcome. Instead, the goal is to choose the option that will lead to the most favorable range of outcomes.

And that's life, isn't it?

It's a never-ending roller coaster. Yet we can all count on one constant—our ability to take control of our own path and rely on our own resilience to lead us through.

If there is one thing I've learned on my journey from poverty to success, it's that self-improvement is something no one can take from you.

And that there's nothing we can't accomplish if we arm ourselves with knowledge, hard work, and a crystal clear vision of the life we want to live.

6. Build systems.

Why do most people set goals and never achieve them? Because most people view their goal as an achievement or failure. This is a conflicting either-or concept. Instead, I propose you develop a systems-first mentality. When you fall in love with the process rather than the outcome, you don't have to give yourself permission to be happy. This isn't to say goals are useless. I believe goals are good for planning your progress, but systems are essential for *making* progress.

I have built systems for every aspect of my life, including raising my children, in my trading career, in my financial advisory business, even in my marriage. A well-designed system will always win, and committing to the process is what makes all the difference. Remember, if you are willing to do the things other people are unwilling to do, eventually you will be able to live the life few can have.

About Ron

Ron Mark has been providing expertise in the financial markets for over three decades, with a concentration in investment strategies, portfolio construction, tax-efficient retirement income planning, and legacy wealth building.

Ron is committed to guiding his clients through the present volatile market, offering tax-free income and life insurance plans, long-term care, and principal protection plans. Ron is passionate about equipping both men and women to ensure they are properly prepared for retirement regarding their assets.

Utilizing his knowledge in insurance and business management, he is devoted to informing, protecting, and educating his customers, allowing them to attain their individual financial and estate objectives. Ron holds a bachelor's degree in finance from the University of Illinois.

Ron holds his Series 65 and Series 3 security licenses and holds Life/ Health licenses. He is a certified Elite POZ Advisor specializing in creating tax-free income streams. Additionally, Ron is a financial educator through the National Society of Financial Educators and a member of the Society for Financial Awareness dedicated to helping pre-retirees improve their lives through comprehensive personal finance education. These courses are conducted on university and college campuses across the country and are designed to increase awareness about financial issues so pre-retirees can make more-informed choices about their retirement. Ron was also previously a board member of the University of Illinois Alumni Association, and of CASL, where he administered finance and risk management tasks. Away from work, Ron enjoys spending time with his family and indulging in hobbies such as martial arts, cooking, traveling, reading books, and golf.

Connect with Ron at rmark@ciacinc.com and https://app.minnect. com/expert/RonMark.

CHAPTER 17

LEVERAGING ATTENTION AS A VEHICLE FOR IMPACT

By Cain Daniel

I t was late.

So late that the streets were completely empty of the normal hustle and bustle, the fog and the quiet creating a bit of an eerie scene as I made my way back to the hostel.

I was in the Netherlands, and though I was unfamiliar with my surroundings, I was surprisingly unafraid of being the sole person on a dimly lit street in a foreign country.

"Need directions?"

A stranger had emerged from around the corner, and though some might mistake his offer as friendly outreach from a local to a traveler, my instincts knew right away that the guy was trouble.

"Wrong guy," I said to let him know I was not about to fall for his false camaraderie and end up being robbed.

I kept walking, only to be intercepted by another man, clearly his partner in this charade.

This guy was brandishing a knife.

At the time, I had a decent amount of money after being paid in cash for the ESL course I'd taught, but stuffed into my sock where I knew no thief was likely to look. In my pocket was a fake wallet holding just a few euros.

"How much do you have?" he asked, turning the blade in his hand as he spoke.

I reached for my decoy wallet, held it up for them to see, and tossed it into the darkness, buying myself a few precious moments to start running to safety.

It was one of the oldest strategies in the book.

Direct attention elsewhere and run!

It worked, and I landed safely in my bed with all two hundred euros still neatly tucked into my sock.

That was years ago, but even today, as vice president of the Real Estate and Mortgage Institute of Canada, I know that capturing and directing attention is the key to influence and impact.

Our mission is to deliver world-class content that helps our students get the licensing they need to get started in the financial services markets and create careers that set them free.

So luckily these days my impact comes from helping our students become entrepreneurs, rather than deterring two thugs from roughing me up!

This is a very important mission for me personally.

I had just started working for a financial institution when my mother, who had just learned she was pregnant with twins, was fired from her job. She's an incredibly strong woman who'd supported my brother and me for most of our childhood. Without any formal education, she had worked her way into the corporate world and did quite well. Her termination was shocking and unjustified.

Seeing her shift from confident and secure to dependent and vulnerable was a huge wake-up call for me.

I decided I didn't want to be at the mercy of any executive team who could decide on a whim to fire me. I made up my mind to empower myself and search for a company that would happily give me more autonomy in my life—while also empowering others to do the same.

So, I quit my job and joined REMIC. Over time I've become a partner at REMIC, not only giving me control over my life but purpose as well. Working to help others become entrepreneurs and create lives of freedom is what drives my ambition.

But I can't help anyone until I have their attention.

SEEING BEYOND THE OBVIOUS

"Look at this," our coach said, hoisting the soccer ball high above his head. "What do you see?" We laughed, thinking it was a trick question. "A soccer ball," we replied in unison. But his response wasn't what we expected.

"No," he said. "This is not a soccer ball. It's a ticket to opportunity, to friendship, to wealth. It's a tool by which your dreams can take flight." In that moment, he wasn't just talking about soccer; he was teaching us the art of thinking bigger and seeing beyond the obvious.

As I ventured into the world of business, I carried that lesson with me.

I stopped looking at a proposal as simply a document outlining a venture. I saw a proposal as a gateway to opportunity, a bridge to new partnerships, and a blueprint for success. Just as the soccer ball symbolized more than a game, a business interaction embodies the potential for growth and abundance.

I may have missed that lesson had my coach not held the ball up high to stop our chatter and grab our attention.

I knew our company could help people temper their tendency to think in black and white. Sure, contracts and licenses matter, but the paper isn't nearly as important as what it represents—in essence, freedom and opportunity!

When a client of ours enters the mortgage industry, they are bombarded with information and complex concepts. Having decades of experience in the industry, we knew we could distill the path to success down to the most important steps, shorten the learning curve, and expedite their personal and professional goals.

We just needed to transcend all the noise and capture their attention.

The art of communication isn't just about words—it's about the ability to command the room and leave an indelible mark.

The question was, How?

IMPACT STARTS WITH INVESTIGATION

Over time my business partner and I noticed that there was a huge influx of people entering the mortgage industry who obviously all planned on getting licensed, but only a quarter of them actually did.

Why was that happening? Where were things breaking down?

We started a lengthy investigative process, researching industry trends and interviewing our target audience to find out what they struggled with the most.

We found that many of them understood how to be a broker but not how to build a profitable business. This prompted us to adopt a mission of transforming our students into entrepreneurs.

We realized that there was a lot of misinformation and a major lack of resources for new agents looking to be business owners. This was a chance for us to serve our audience at a much higher level and deliver services we believed could change lives.

After some research, we found that there wasn't a solid forum for brokers, new and seasoned, to talk to one another, ask questions, or get help.

But with so much noise and saturation, we knew we needed a platform. After all, we couldn't help anyone until we had their attention.

We developed a social media app, branded it, and pushed it out just to brokers and agents. Within the first year our audience grew to more than twenty-five hundred members. In the confines of that space, we have a captive audience and act as the primary voice of expertise.

Attention is the bridge to impact.

There's a science to creating and leading a captive audience, but it's a simple formula that anyone can learn. And it's one that gives you the kind of built-in authority you need to help your audience achieve success.

THE POWER OF GROUP IDENTITY

The air is hazy with smoke, the grounds covered in a sea of psychedelic tie-dye, and the audience sways back and forth, arms around each other in warmth and kinship, proud to be a part of this like-minded group, the Deadheads.

The Grateful Dead has one of the most loyal followings in the world. Audiences travel show to show in a shared spirit of peace, love, and rock and roll. The Grateful Dead never worried about ticket sales. They knew the Deadheads would show up.

Across town a tight-knit community of fit bodies and fierce minds sweat through their workouts, pushing each other to personal limits and celebrating every rep. CrossFit enthusiasts have forged their group identity in sweat and determination, proud of their badges as fitness warriors.

If you want to capture attention, group identity is a must. It serves as the foundation for communication and collective growth. When you and the people you serve find common purpose, there is a natural tendency toward camaraderie and trust.

It starts with self-reflection. You've got to know your (or your business's) values, strengths, beliefs, and aspirations. You've got to know what you're striving for. You definitely have to know how you are unique and better than all the other available options.

Once you have a clear sense of your identity, you've got to communicate it boldly and widely in a way that others can recognize and relate to. The more you tell your story and declare your values and goals, the more likely your ideal clients will find you and choose to join your world.

Once they are in, you can lead them toward a shared sense of unity and purpose, steering everyone involved toward a collective vision for a brighter future.

Establishing identity is not just about defining your brand; it's about creating a sense of belonging and purpose that resonates with others. When people see themselves in your group dynamic, they are more likely to pay attention, engage with your message, and ultimately, be influenced by your ideas.

MAKE MORE DEPOSITS THAN WITHDRAWALS

One of the general rules of marketing and influence is the 80/20 rule. The idea is that 80 percent of the time, you should be offering value, teaching or entertaining, leaving only 20 percent for sales and calls to action.

I like to think of it as deposits and withdrawals.

In our community we strive to make deposits of value every day. We offer advice; we give training; we answer questions. We do so much of it that when we do have an offer to make, it is well received.

Whether you're managing a group or interacting one-to-one, provide value first.

Be a resource. Be careful not to think transactionally, because people sense that. Instead, build your own positioning as a thought leader who provides genuine value tailored to the needs and interests of your audience, whether your audience is two or two thousand.

Providing value is step one to establishing trust and credibility. It's essential to approach every interaction with a spirit of generosity instead of focusing solely on your own agenda.

When people see that you are genuinely invested in their success, they are more likely to listen to what you have to say and be open to taking the action you want them to take.

Let's say you're trying to close a deal with a vendor. Do your research. Maybe before the meeting even takes place, you send them a helpful news article. Maybe you share some news you heard that could affect their industry, or share a contact you think could help them with that tech problem they mentioned.

Make deposits before you make withdrawals.

LEAD WITH A GOAL FOR EMPATHY AND COLLABORATION

Whether it's a social media app, a community forum, a meeting room in an office building, or a group chat, provide an environment that serves as a gathering place where like-minded people (all your intended audience) come together to share ideas and information and build relationships.

The key is to create an energy that fosters engagement and participation. You've got their attention, so you want to make sure you hold on to it by facilitating meaningful conversations.

One of the most common mistakes I see business professionals making is that they work hard and spend a great deal of their budget to get their prospect's attention, and then get lazy about keeping it.

When you build a group identity, you do so to create a sense of shared purpose, which leads to collaboration over competition.

Most importantly, you create a secure place in which your prospect can expect grace and empathy, making them more likely to share and take action.

Ultimately, providing a platform is about empowering others to find their voice and make a difference in the world. By creating a space where people can come together to collaborate and cocreate, you can harness the collective power of community to drive positive change and create a better future for all involved.

As we listened to the inaugural members of our app, we uncovered new challenges and opportunities for growth. They vented about a need; we stepped in and filled the gap. They asked a question; we created a resource that answered it. They offered an idea; we were willing to try it.

The more your audience feels seen, heard, and cared for, the more loyal they become.

Loyalty is a cornerstone of influence.

Just ask the Grateful Dead.

Twenty-five years after lead singer Jerry Garcia's death, the Deadheads still gather to listen to tribute bands. They still wear their teddy bear T-shirts, and they're still toasting the guy who started it all.

Imagine the kind of impact we could all have if we inspired that much devotion and mobilized it for the greater good.

THE FAST TRACK TO CAPTURING ATTENTION

When I was a kid, my family moved around a lot.

In fact, I attended a different school for every single year of elementary school.

As you can imagine, it wasn't easy always being the new kid. I had to get creative and find ways to insert myself into established groups. If I didn't, I would be invisible.

I learned that there was one strategy that instantly captured attention and got me noticed: questions.

People love to talk about themselves and demonstrate their expertise. Where did you get those shoes? Who is the worst teacher? Who is the best teacher?

I found that when I lurked around, I didn't get very far, but when I asked a question, kids were eager to talk!

As I entered the business world, navigating marketing, negotiations, and contracts, I realized that curiosity is a strategy that works at any age. Humans, young and old, like to talk about themselves.

Every one of us has a story, a set of values, passionate goals, and lifelong dreams, and we tend to light up at the opportunity to share them.

Whether I'm creating a new offer, looking to influence a buying decision, or trying to solve a client's problem, I find that the more questions I ask, the more successful I am.

Questions open the door to influence. When someone is answering your question, their attention is fixed on you. Which is the perfect opportunity for you to ask *more* questions, to mirror their response, establish trust, and ultimately guide the interaction to a mutually beneficial end.

As I look back on my journey, it all started on the soccer field with one simple question: "What do you see?"

That question taught me to go beyond the surface. To dig deeper. To broaden my thinking.

When I meet with a new client, I don't just see a person. I see potential. For me and for them. I see possibilities for abundance and freedom.

I see our agreement not as paper and ink but as a vehicle by which I can make the impact I want to make so that they can live the life they want to live.

About Cain

With over a decade of leadership in professional education, Cain Daniel has helped thousands of entrepreneurs break into and excel in the financial services industry. As a business leader, he has demonstrated success in sales, marketing, operations, and the development of innovative strategies.

Cain is a partner and serves as vice president at REMIC, a leading educational institute for financial services throughout Canada. He has also cofounded AMIPROS, an association dedicated to educating mortgage professionals and the public about investing in mortgages.

Cain is driven by his mission to transform students into successful entrepreneurs. His passion for innovative training has equipped individuals with the essential tools and strategies necessary to achieve success in their entrepreneurial journeys.

Outside the office, Cain channels his competitive spirit into playing soccer and enjoys his downtime with his wife and their two children, Mila and Evan.

You can learn more at caindaniel.com or remic.ca.

CHAPTER 18

TO MAKE AN IMPACT, GET OUT OF YOUR OWN WAY!

By Alen Rakipovic

stood at the football pitch and watched with disappointment as my team conceded yet another goal. We were down three goals with twenty minutes left to play. It felt as if there was no point in pushing to turn the result around. My teammates had their heads down, slumped in defeat. "We can't win this."

A moment later I realized that my mind was sabotaging me and the team. I wiped the sweat from my face, regrouped the team, gave them a new play strategy, a vision of how we could win, and reorganized the players. We made a comeback and won the game.

I was happy we won. What mattered more was how I felt when a teammate approached me after and said he had never seen anyone turn around a team in such a positive way and that he appreciated my refusal to give up on winning.

This is one of thousands of times when my own assumptions and emotions almost got in the way of my goals. For more than a decade I have been working as a technology leader, building software organizations in consumer tech and finance for some of the biggest, most well-known companies in the world.

Over time I felt myself becoming increasingly needy, stressed, and fixated on the next win. The turning point came when a complex project negotiation at work collapsed and negatively influenced our family time for months. What I really needed, and wanted to return to, was a positive influence and impact on others and long-term outcomes.

I cultivated the discipline to recognize when I was getting in my own way with ego or needs that were really wants or faulty assumptions. And even more critical, I learned to recognize when I was not seeing or listening to where others were coming from. If I leave you with anything, it's this: Influence and impact depend first on self-awareness.

This way of thinking is available to anyone—it's a skill and needs consistent practice. Here are three steps to fostering a sense of self-awareness as a bridge to impact an influence. I had to learn to release baggage, get motivated by quiet success, and make differences count.

RELEASE YOUR BAGGAGE

During a high-stakes project, I faced a difficult negotiation when a partner software team informed us that they wouldn't make the public release deadline. There were delays in building machine learning models, a factor that's crucial to the project's success, and it seemed as if we were stuck without a solution.

To understand their process and find a way forward, I asked our team to meet with them. We discovered that their manual validation process was consuming a significant amount of their time, but the real discovery was that this part of the process could be incorporated into our existing data pipeline.

My initial assumption was that the only way to meet the deadline was to take complete ownership of the validation process from the partner team.

The problem was that the partner team leader was hesitant to relinquish control over any part of it. And my approach would only create the opposite effect. I was being driven by baggage— not trusting some of the team from previous experience and assuming if I took complete ownership, success was guaranteed, because that's how I had succeeded on many things in the past. I felt as if I *needed* to be in control of everything—an irrational but enticing view.

I shifted my focus to understanding the views of the other team so that I could define a way for us to collaborate on solving the problem.

They had put months of work into this project, and here I was, asking them to trust me to step in and mess with it! I knew I could help, though. I have a gift for finding ways to consolidate resources and reorganize teams, so I felt there were ways to persuade the team's leadership to work with us.

They visited our office, and during that meeting we went through the details of their validations, processes, and ideas of how to proceed, and their expectations and ideas about what to do next. I shared data about validations my team had done. The quality of the data on our side matched theirs, which turned out to be one of their main concerns and was now completely addressed.

Rather than persuading them to accept my way forward, we engaged in a *dialogue* aimed at uncovering underlying needs, concerns, and objectives. By actively listening and empathizing with the other party's perspective, we found a common vision. To even take this approach, I had to let go of my baggage.

We worked together and saved 20 percent of machine learning model building time, which enabled us to launch the project on time with great success. This approach was risky for my team because in using our resources to help this team, we had a higher chance of missing our *own* deadlines, but I decided to take the risk because I saw a way to reorganize the team, leverage our different skill sets, and speed up our overall project delivery time.

My neediness to want to be in control, along with the assumption of a single possibility forward, could have cost us missing the public launch deadline. This was avoided, by first setting my focus on learning to embrace the present moment, and the endless possibilities it offered, not just the solution that fed my ego. Samurais do this—in the moment of tension, they fully focus, widening their peripheral vision to see open areas to strike next. They have a much greater chance of succeeding if they quiet distraction and focus on the sword!

GET MOTIVATED BY QUIET SUCCESS

I love football. I have played it my entire life, and lessons from the playing field sometimes strongly mirror other areas of life. On the football pitch, it matters that the captain can influence the team. They are the connective tissue between all the players, coaches, club's leadership, referees, and fans. They can go unnoticed but remain highly motivated to drive the team's success.

The analogy came back to me while working with a finance company. They had been in business for many decades, and were highly successful and fairly set in their ways of operating, but they wanted more of the benefits of new technology to drive their business.

To make this happen, they hired me and a team of other big-tech leaders. Our first mistake was thinking we could run this initiative without the legacy tech group involved. Eventually, we found ourselves at a critical juncture when we needed their help with company-wide implementation.

Without their cooperation we were at a standstill.

I began to work extra hard to facilitate a connection between my team and the technology department. It was working, but I found myself growing frustrated that my efforts were not recognized, and I found myself in a very negative mental state. When I went home at the end of the day, I brought that frustration with me.

The antidote to my frustration—a mindset-shifting phrase I happened to be reminded of on social media: "You can accomplish anything if you don't take the credit." A switch flipped. I decided to let go of wanting recognition. Instead, I decided to focus on building relationships and cultivating a great work environment. The teams began working well together, even having fun, and I was actually relaxed at the end of the workday.

Oddly, it was when I stopped needing recognition that I started to receive it! I was offered a promotion a short time after.

I have an innate gift for building bridges between people and teams. I have made a bigger impact on many things when I was willing to use that gift and not get shortsighted or thrown by the need for recognition.

MAKE DIFFERENCES COUNT

In primary school I started participating in math competitions and did quite well. I became a top competitor in my county but not anywhere else! By high school I would look at the results of national math competitions and ask myself, "How are these people so brilliant?" They were solving equations I hadn't even seen!

My view of the world was limited to my small hometown, where possibilities were scarce and the idea of math as a field of study was not widely popularized.

No one came to my school to give a lecture on math, and there was never an opportunity to learn from or connect to people outside of my town. From there, I went to the capital to attend university and study computer science. It turns out that those same brilliant people, whose scores I had marveled at, were going to school there too. Not only did I meet those people, but we became best friends.

After weeks of discussion and getting to know each other, it became clear to us that children in more remote parts of Croatia were missing opportunities to learn and compete in math simply because of their location and a lack of resources.

We decided to start a nonprofit with the mission of working with young, talented mathematicians to help them cultivate innovative ideas, establish math as a field of study in which they could participate, and open the doors to new friendships with like-minded people. Two main projects were to organize weekly lectures across the country to prepare talented students for mathematics competitions, and to host a summer camp to connect young mathematicians from various cities.

It worked!

It has been more than a decade since we started that organization, and since then, hundreds of students have been through our math camps and lectures. Croatia had competed in national math competitions before but had always peaked at a silver medal. After attending our math camps and lectures, Croatian students won the gold and went on to win many medals in International Mathematical Olympiads. More importantly, they built friendships for life.

Also know that it almost didn't work. We had heated debates and differences of opinion about how to incentivize lecturers to participate. We debated on whether to pay them. If we pay them, why would they come back when the money was not huge? If we didn't pay them, how would we get enough quality lecturers? Which model would help the community grow and live on long term?

In retrospect, negotiating through our different views on this topic turned out to be the most critical aspect of the program's long success. We decided not to pay lecturers. It has resulted in a community with a high sense of duty, who keep coming back. Students become lecturers, and the lecturers return because the results are impressive when they do.

Was this a success? Well, none of us made any money from this endeavor. Not a penny. But it was wildly successful in its mission and taught me to cultivate the mindset of making differences count. By negotiating through differences of opinion, what looks like a conflict or being stuck can turn into a positive, high-value way forward. We had to get out of our own way of thinking and work together to solve the mission.

To this day I am most proud to have been a part of this team. It required me to step out of my view of limitations and scarce possibilities and truly embrace the idea that I could make an impact on kids while working alongside some of the most brilliant minds out there.

What I have found to be true with my tech teams, with the math nonprofit, and with my family is that influence and impact compound when you listen to others; find a cohesive vision, leverage your most unique gifts, and most importantly...

Get out of your own way!

About Alen

Alen Rakipovic was shaped most in his view of leadership as a teenager in his father's family business. He saw his father relentlessly build on the legacy of his father but with a unique quality. His father has a way about him that makes people, his customers, volunteer to do things for him, and happily. This is Alen's strongest imprint of influence and persuasion.

From this world he ventured into technology companies, where he built software organizations in consumer tech and asset management, including Amazon, Meta, and Capital Group. These roles exposed him to a diverse set of challenges, such as machine translation, AI, investment risk management, and advertising tech. He has led teams across three continents and seven countries.

Alen is passionate about leveling the playing field with technology and education. He is an adviser to several early-stage companies and investor. His career mission is to build technologies that positively impact people's lives and to build teams that laugh.

To connect with Alen, feel free to reach out on LinkedIn: www.linkedin.com/in/arakipovic.

CHAPTER 19

THE NEGOTIATOR'S EDGE

By Ryan Rackley

The negotiation room exuded a palpable tension that seemed to hang in the air. I could feel the sweat forming on my face, and my instincts, usually strong and standing at the ready, were becoming diluted by the minute.

Across the table the opposition, a formidable force, held her ground, her jaw tightening in resistance. For a moment there was a silent stalemate, the hum of the air conditioning providing the soundtrack for this familiar high-stakes gamble.

As a seasoned contract negotiator, I had navigated these waters before. The negotiation room, to me, was a comfortable space where I had thrived, relishing the tightrope balance between risk and reward. This was my arena, so it was frustrating to feel myself losing ground.

This particular negotiation room was my kitchen. The opponent, my adorable eleven-year-old daughter. It was her birthday, and she wanted to rent a boat for a half day to go tubing with friends, then take them all to a water park, and *then* host them all for a sleepover. I was tired just thinking about it.

I attempted to negotiate, to persuade her to think of something else she'd like to do, but that's when my zero-leverage kicked in. All she had to do was bat her eyes at me, give me a couple of guilt-based one-liners, and I caved in less than ten minutes.

I had to ask myself, as all professionals should, "Where did I go wrong?" Well, I hadn't brought a plan B to the table, hadn't prepared well enough, had allowed my emotions to get the best of me, and had essentially abandoned all the strategies and tactics that had helped me build a very successful career.

The end result was amazing, and we had a great day. I'd be lying if I said I wouldn't do it all over again.

But it did get me thinking...

Life is an ongoing negotiation, in which we all navigate a complex and never-ending web of decisions, choices, and interactions. Each day we are presented with a series of challenges, usually involving other people with opposing points of view, and we must find a way to live in harmony. We have to balance empathy with leadership, adapt to unexpected curveballs, and keep our cool, all while searching for outcomes that are mutually beneficial.

If we learn to do it well, we can enjoy a solid and fulfilling career path and healthy, joyful relationships. If we don't do it well, life is an uphill and lonely battle.

As a partner at Cornerstone Advisors, I lead a team of highly specialized technology contract negotiation consultants in the firm's negotiation solution group. I've spent more than twenty years in the financial services space and personally negotiated more than five hundred bank and credit union technology contracts.

I've been witness to insanely tense and dramatic negotiations where fortunes and reputations were lost. And I've led successful negotiations in which both sides ultimately benefited, and millions of dollars were both won and saved at the same time, depending on which side of the table your seat was on.

It's all fairly predictable. If you want to be an influential person and accomplish big goals, there are things to do and ways of being that exponentially increase your chances of doing so.

Over the years I have honed a formula for successful persuasion that has served me well, and having taught it to hundreds of others, I can confidently say it's a formula that works in any type of negotiation, whether your opponent is a staunch and unyielding CEO or a convincing little girl with sparkling brown eyes and just the right blend of strength and sweetness.

KNOWING WHERE YOU ARE GOING IS THE
FIRST STEP TO GETTING THERE

I'll never forget this day as long as I live.

I was floating in my pool with a margarita, because that's what we do in Arizona, when I got a phone call that would alter the trajectory of my entire life.

I had been working as a consultant, and one of my clients was a small community institution working to negotiate their technology contract. After spending some time weeding through their files, I realized they had been getting crushed by their current contract, which had been in place (and had gone unchecked) for nearly twenty-five years!

At this point I had gotten to know this team well, and the thought that they had been massively overpaying was curdling my stomach. I couldn't live with the knowledge that these hard-working salt-of-the-earth people were being taken for a ride and no one was looking out for them.

So I took it to the negotiation table.

I needed to win this. Millions of dollars were at stake. I prepared for weeks, identified where we wanted to go, armed myself with data on the pricing gap, and had a solid timeline in mind of when we needed this to be resolved. When it was over, we cut their costs by 85 percent. They were stunned. They had no idea going in that there was an 85 percent cost opportunity to negotiate. A couple of weeks later I got a call on a Friday night from the CEO of the institution, who lived on the East Coast. I was in the pool having a margarita, and when I saw the caller ID, I couldn't imagine what was coming. Why would the CEO call me at 10:30 EST on a Friday night?

I answered the phone, and he said, "Ryan, I have to tell you this. You didn't know this, but you saved this entire bank from certain failure. We were on the brink. The work you did bought me eighteen months to turn this around. So on behalf of the five hundred families depending on me to keep their livelihoods afloat, thank you."

I knew in that blink of a moment that this would be my career. I realized the far-reaching impact I could have using persuasive communication and effective negotiation skills, which is a skill anyone can learn.

But you've got to begin by knowing what you want. In that case, I wanted to renegotiate an unfair and outdated contract, and I wasn't going to back down until a new contract was presented that was nothing short of highly competitive.

Once you have a destination in mind, you can reverse-engineer the process, figure out what success would look like, and map out digestible steps toward your goal.

It doesn't matter if your goal is to lead a merger, lose weight, or write a book—you can't get anywhere if you don't know where you're going.

"You Don't Get What You Deserve; You Get What You Negotiate"

Those were the words of Chester Karrass, creator of the most successful negotiation seminar in the country.

They are also words that my parents would agree with.

I come from a family of entrepreneurs, and I started working in our family businesses at the ripe age of eight. I could understand from a young age that most things don't happen by accident and not everything is fair. And I learned that if you want something, you've got to work for it, fight for it, negotiate for it.

Whether I was selling something to a customer in our family business or presenting an argument for why I should be allowed to borrow the car, I understood that one of the biggest indicators of influence is preparation.

A lack of preparation is a sign of entitlement. When someone is unwilling to do the work to prepare for something, it stems from a predisposed expectation of success. They believe they are inherently deserving of a win regardless of whether they have earned it through hard work and diligence.

My father would never have gone for that!

You must prepare in order to persuade.

If you don't, you show up entitled and unprepared, and you automatically concede the upper hand.

A while back I got a call from a guy who was deadlocked in a negotiation over a contract that was expiring in just twelve days. He hadn't prepared, hadn't allowed enough time, and because of that had to resort to what I call Emergency Reaction Mode, which often translates as an ego-driven emotional outburst. Desperate people tend to think that talking louder gives them authority when what it actually does is show their weakness.

When I witness someone in Emergency Reaction Mode, I instantly know that they are unprepared and frantic, which means I am much more likely to get the outcome I want.

In negotiations, we use angles and levers. Angles are strategies deployed to persuade the other party to consider my point of view. Levers are resources I have at my disposal, such as pricing knowledge and alternative options, that give me leverage. When the other side of the table is pounding their fists and shouting demands, I pull out my angles and levers because I know now that they don't have any!

I stepped in to help him and was glad I did. He would have been overpaying by 40 percent for the next five years, all because his ego took over and he was being lazy.

So, What Does It Mean to Prepare to Persuade?

As I said before, you've got to know what you want. But you've also got to know what *they* want. What is the ROI that both sides are going for? What's the break-even point?

Have you gathered enough information to establish a position of knowledge? Are you prepared with leverage?

For instance, have you gathered crucial information, market

insights or data not available to the other party that you can use as a persuasive edge?

And perhaps most importantly, what's your plan B?

You might remember that I lost a high-stakes negotiation with my daughter because I had not prepared an alternative to offer her.

You've got to show up with an alternative. Notice I said "alternative," not compromise.

WIN-WIN SCENARIOS ARE AN EASY BUTTON NONE OF US SHOULD PUSH!

There is a common misconception that compromise is key. The dictionary definition of the word *compromise* is "an agreement of a dispute that is reached by both sides making concessions."

What that means, essentially, is that both sides end up with less than they hoped for.

Identifying what is acceptable and nonnegotiable before taking your seat at the table comes first.

Don't go to win, win and meet in the middle too fast.

Know your nonnegotiables, and don't believe what your adversary tells you are theirs.

Two parties have diverging objectives and eventually, win-win people often experience buyer's remorse because neither side did their homework; they agree to "meet in the middle."

Now of course, in a true negotiation the outcome does have to be acceptable to both parties.

But if you've ever been in a relationship in which your partner concedes to meet in the middle, you know that the middle can be a breeding ground for resentment, and whatever unmet need lingers is bound to show up again and again during an argument!

Regardless of the situation you're in, the ideal scenario is that both sides are mature and professional enough to understand that the win-win may not always lie at the perfect midpoint.

This is when you need to get curious and creative! Tap into your empathy and be genuinely curious about what the other party needs and wants. Remember, what they want, what they need, and what they've been programmed to ask for could all be different things, so you have to cultivate a gift for reading between the lines and asking good questions.

The new goal shifts to forming an outcome that creates value for both sides and is more expansive than a compromise. Instead of dividing the pie so that everyone ends up with less, we enlarge the pie so that everyone benefits *more*.

This kind of collaborative approach allows both sides to hold on to some decision-making power, and that's what we want. When drama and competition are defused, everyone becomes more open to a change in perspective resulting in the outcome you need.

Amateurs approach persuasion through a lens of "me versus you."

Pros, while trained to get what they want, never do that. It's never "me against you," but rather "us against the problem...and the clock."

Light Bulb Moment

When I was about twenty years old, my dad was getting ready to retire and had begun to wind down the family businesses. He sold a couple of them and closed another, and I felt terrible for him. He had poured his whole life into these businesses, and now the doors were closing, the shelves would be emptied, and pretty soon everything he worked for would just be a memory.

I remember feeling so sorry for him. This just didn't seem like the outcome he would want. I went to him and said, "Dad, I'm so sorry you're going through this. I'm sorry it didn't work." He took me aside and he said, "You don't understand. You've got it all wrong. This is a major success! It's how you define it that matters."

He went on to talk about all the people he had helped along the way and the amazing relationships he had built in the community. Then he said, "Here's the thing about the money—I don't need it!

We're good. We've done well enough, and we are surrounded by people we've helped."

My mind was blown. To that point, I had always defined success by how much one can get and *keep* getting. That day changed the way I engaged with success.

Today, despite the fact that I still pride myself on being the guy people call when millions of dollars are at stake, I have shifted my definition of winning.

Winning to me can be summed up as this:

- making a far-reaching impact through my work,

- showing up with the intent to collaborate,

- leaning in to a genuine and never-ending curiosity about people and what makes them tick, and

- building relationships that leave a mark.

That CEO who interrupted my pool time to thank me for saving his bank? We still talk. For ten years we've acted as one another's confidant and sounding board.

People and relationships are the foundation and cornerstone of success.

Wherever you are trying to make an impact, I hope you'll remember that true victory lies where desires and aspirations converge.

Much like two stars crashing into one another creates a brighter star, lasting impact forms at the intersection where collaborative goals collide to produce far-reaching influence and game-changing results.

About Ryan

Ryan Rackley, a seasoned professional negotiator with over twenty-five years' experience, is devoted to advocating for those at the negotiation table where the deck is stacked against them. Ryan's careful preparation, tireless efforts, laser-focused intensity, passionate dedication to making a positive difference, unique skills for conflict resolution, and ongoing quest and thirst for knowledge and skills within the human influence arena have shaped his career.

Ryan's career path is unique. He spent the initial part of his career working within a regional bank acquiring an in-depth understanding of operations and technology modernization, and a foundational understanding of the application of power and influence. Then, Ryan spent many years on the architecture and sales side of the negotiation table. The experience gained from "the other side" of the table has proved invaluable, engraining a deep sense of empathy and understanding of the pressures of negotiations from all angles. Now, Ryan is able to take everything he has learned over his career and apply it to the large B2B negotiating environment, enabling amazing outcomes for his client, producing results, combining and creatively applying angles, levers, and influence at the table, resulting in winning narratives.

Currently a partner at a prestigious boutique management consulting firm, Ryan leads and mentors a team of highly specialized technology contract negotiation consultants. Ryan has personally negotiated more than five hundred major bank and credit union technology contracts, creating billions in measurable outcomes at the negotiation table. He is now operating at scale, serving a critical need to maintain the health of an entire industry.

Ryan evangelizes his concepts and leads discussions regularly for industry webinars, executive roundtables, and a named white paper author, and is a sought-after speaker at industry conferences.

Ryan holds a certification of Executive Presence and Leadership from The Wharton School, twelve technical certifications, a master of business administration degree, and a bachelor of arts degree in computer science from the prestigious Washburn University.

Connect with Ryan: www.linkedin.com/in/rackley-ryan.

CHAPTER 20

THE POWER OF QUIET PERSUASION

By Sheryl Driggers

"I'm sorry to be the one to tell you this, but you have a rare genetic disorder. And whatever you do...don't google it."

The air left the room. The doctor continued to talk, but her voice now seemed distant and muffled, and all I could hear was the hum of the fluorescent lights overhead and the anxious beating of my heart.

I didn't know what retinitis pigmentosa was, but I couldn't shake the chilling sense that everything was about to change.

Words like *serious* and *specialist* fell from the doctor's lips.

The room seemed to sway, and mentally, a storm of thoughts and emotions collided,

Of course, I left the office and immediately did what I was told not to do; I googled. The search results were long and complex, but one line seemed magnified as everything around it blurred: *leads to vision loss.*

I was going to go blind.

I sat there for a long time staring at the screen, the comfort of everyday life splintering, and wrestled with the reality that this diagnosis would redefine the course of my life.

At that moment, I experienced a confusing blend of terror and gratitude. Terror of the unknown, but gratitude for the large and caring support system around me of family, friends, and coworkers who would rally to support my journey.

And that hadn't always been the case.

My husband, Jason, and I were married in 2000, and after a few chaotic years in the corporate world, we were anxious to start something new together.

A friend in the collision repair industry made us aware of a shop location that was going out of business. Neither of us had ever even considered entering the collision repair industry, but the profit margins were great, and before we knew it, we had purchased the building and started a new business!

Shortly after that we were blessed with two kids, a son and a daughter, and by 2017 we were opening our third location.

If it sounds like a whirlwind, it was. I was caring for two small children while spending days learning all aspects of the collision repair business, eager to soak up as much as I could about our industry.

For the first ten-plus years of my career as a shop owner, I led from a singular focus on results, KPIs, and task completion. I strove for perfection in everything I did, and I expected the same out of my team. My priorities at the time were well out of focus, but I had no idea. We were growing, and I mistakenly credited it to my bullheaded and rigid leadership approach, which involved setting increasingly high standards for excellence for every member of the team.

One day a team member in one of our locations made a mistake. I immediately fired off a pretty threatening email to that employee and copied the entire staff on it. I was proud of how quickly I had managed the situation until a colleague said to me, "Sheryl, you owe all of them an apology."

Later that night as I was telling my husband about the situation, he said something to me that I'll never forget. He said, "Sheryl, I don't think you have any idea how you talk to people."

What was happening? We were succeeding, the shops were profitable, and on paper everything was going exactly as it should, and yet two people I respected were calling me out on how I was making that happen. While not entirely convinced of their perspective at that moment, my respect for them prompted me to embark on a journey of transformation and leadership.

I picked up a copy of the book *The 7 Habits of Highly Effective People* by Stephen Covey. In it there is an exercise that prompts you to write down what people might say about you at your funeral.

That exercise wrecked me.

I thought about what my children would say, and the first thing that came to mind was, "Nothing was ever good enough for her." I thought about what my employees would say and realized that most of them would likely say, "She was a dictator, always yelling and putting everyone down. The shop felt like a constant stress zone because of her."

Have you ever had a moment of truly seeing yourself for the first time, your flaws and mistakes held up in front of you like a merciless mirror that allows you to see yourself the way others see you? It's not pretty. That moment marked a huge turning point for me.

I decided that from that day on I would treat people differently. I would be the person they admired, not feared. I would lead my children with love, not criticism. I would make our collision repair shops happy and inspiring places to work.

And I would do it without saying a word.

THE ART OF QUIET PERSUASION

There's a common misconception, and one I led with for years, that to persuade anyone to do what you want them to do, you must use words. Urgent words. Aggressive words. *Loud* words.

I know now that if you have to *demand* respect, you probably aren't worthy of it.

What many people don't realize is that masterful persuasion happens without a sound. It happens by way of inspired action. I had yelled enough. Now I was determined to create significant influence on others through a calm presence that *earned* respect.

Quiet persuasion holds a power that transcends verbal

communication. It utilizes actions, energy, and subtle cues to shape perceptions and influence others. This form of persuasion operates on a deeper, more intuitive level. I knew that my demeanor, work ethic, and overall energy could convey messages that resonated far beyond a harshly spoken word.

This was a major aha moment! In my experience bosses tended to focus on measurable systems and processes, ignoring the fact that they were in fact employing *humans*. I don't know about you, but as an adult human I have never responded well to being intimidated or condescended to.

When I shifted my method of persuasion from, "How do I get them to do what I want?" to "How can I inspire them to enthusiastically succeed?" our business grew exponentially, and our faith and family dynamic expanded and deepened in a way I could not have imagined.

What I learned is that what begins internally, projects externally. Company culture is defined as the living, breathing persona of your company. Family culture is the living, breathing persona of your household. If you can create a culture of joy and excellence wherever you are, everyone around you will naturally strive to help you preserve it.

And the best part? It's a practice that builds your bank account, feeds your soul, and is readily available to anyone willing to lay down their armor and follow the steps.

CREATE A CULTURE OF COMMUNITY

Leaders do indeed have a responsibility to care for people and deliver excellence. These goals are not the opposite of each other; they complement one another. However, there is a priority, and if you get that wrong, you start running off the rails in all other areas.

I spent too many years focused solely on the bottom line and perfection.

People are always the priority.

Without people you have no business! Without *fulfilled* people you might have a business, but the weight of dysfunction will drag your numbers down and eventually be evident to your customers!

In 2023 the US Surgeon General released an eighty-page advisory report that sent shock waves through the nation. It wasn't about a new disease outbreak or a groundbreaking medical discovery but highlighted a silent and growing crisis: loneliness. The report revealed that loneliness is as detrimental to physical health as smoking a staggering fifteen cigarettes a day. This revelation under-scores the importance of creating a sense of community within the workplace so that the "office" becomes a refuge and support system.

Never was this more important than after my diagnosis. I had been diagnosed in 2015, and by 2019 I had lost the ability to drive.

This impacted my entire family. I was the one who took the kids to school and to extracurricular activities. Losing that ability was a huge blow. I desperately missed our morning routine, as those morning drives were always the time the kids were most talkative and open about what was going on in their lives. Having that taken from me was devastating. I could no longer participate in the things like grocery shopping and the other things it takes to run a household. I could no longer drive myself to work or pop into the shops to visit my team members, at least not without asking for assistance.

Our team members were incredibly supportive. I'm horrible at asking for help, but it is one of the (many) things God has been working on in me. Had I not done the work years earlier to change my ways and foster a sense of community, I'm not sure I would have had the same level of support from my family and team that I am blessed with now.

The bottom line is that people will make mistakes. People will get sick. Even your best employee will have off days, and if you can respond with empathy to these situations, you will find that your employees will be grateful.

And gratitude is a stronger motivator than yelling will ever be!

CREATE A CULTURE OF PURPOSE AND TRANSPARENCY

"I'm the boss; you're the employee." That was my perspective when I first became a business owner. I would march through the shops, shoulders back and head high, every click of my high heels acting as a warning signal to the employees to look sharp!

I made the rules. I called the shots.

What I didn't understand at that time is that people perform better when they believe they play an essential role in the organization's success.

Typically, the people "on the front lines" have valuable insights into how business can improve. I learned to open the lines of communication and demonstrate that I valued their input. If people see the relationship between their contribution and the team's success, they will feel a sense of purpose, which sets off a feel-good ripple effect of dopamine and inspires them to keep working hard and generating good ideas!

Back then we would send out weekly KPI reports to all team members and spend ten minutes each week going over the scores with the entire team. When you see a performance gap, it is easy to apply more pressure to your team to reach the target. However, I learned that the pressure tactic usually caused people to go backward or quit. When I started instead to coach my team and ask for their input on how to fill the gaps, I found it was a much more effective approach.

This commitment to mining the wisdom of our team led to *engaged* team members who now had a greater sense of purpose and direction. An engaged team member is just as important as, if not more important than, an engaged customer. If you have employees who are not engaged, or worse, actively *disengaged*, they are draining the life out of the organization.

A Gallup research study indicates that companies with a highly engaged workforce outperform their peers by 147 percent in earnings per share.

That's the magic of communication, purpose, and quiet persuasion.

A Culture of Giving

In January 2010 my husband and I were sitting in an airport, waiting for a flight and watching the news as a disastrous 7.0 magnitude earthquake hit Haiti, killing over 160,000 people and displacing nearly 1.5 million people.

Have you ever been so moved by something that you are called to action even though doing so defies all logic? That was this moment for me. I could hear the voice of God loud and clear. I turned to Jason and told him I was going to Haiti for disaster relief. Though I had never traveled outside of the US and didn't even have a passport—he supported me.

Two weeks later I was in Haiti.

Seeing the devastation and the families desperate for basic necessities awakened something inside me, and I knew that giving back would now be a cornerstone of our lives and company culture.

About a year after I returned home, Jason's grandfather passed away, leaving us determined to carry on a famous legacy he had in his community. Every season around Christmas, Jason's granddaddy would set up a barbecue on his front lawn and give a meal to whomever needed it.

So, in December 2012 we did the same thing in our shop's parking lot. We anticipated twenty or thirty people initially. Instead, hundreds of needy people flooded our shop.

I was blown away that so many people right in my own community didn't have access to basic necessities. That was the beginning of the The James 215 Project.

Founded in 2013, The James 215 Project is based on the Bible verse James 2:15. The mission of the organization is to know the needs of the community and fill them.

For several years we held this event partnering with other nonprofits and the Florida Department of Children and Families to provide five hundred backpacks, prefilled with an outfit, to adults and children in need.

Our employees were granted fifty-two volunteer hours each year, which equates to one hour per week. That hour per week is paid.

When people feel like they are a part of something special, they raise their level of generosity and productivity in an effort to preserve their role in the shared mission.

Once again, quiet persuasion for the win.

LOVE SPEAKS LOUDER THAN WORDS

True influence is impossible without relationships, and relationships do not develop without being intentional.

We can get so caught up in all the tasks that must be accomplished that we leave little or no room in our calendar to develop our *relationships*.

As Jon Gordon writes in his book *Soup: A Recipe to Nourish Your Team and Culture*, "Businesses that delivered legendary service also had the strongest, most supportive cultures in which employees were valued, listened to, cared for, served, appreciated and loved; in turn, these employees valued, cared for, served, appreciated, and loved the organization."

As human beings we all need to feel seen and appreciated. My husband and I have been "scorned" on more than one occasion because of the level of relationships we have with our team members. We have been told not to get close to people because they will take advantage of the relationship. However, we have found just the opposite.

We've come to realize that true leadership does not require authoritative persuasion; rather, it thrives when people are naturally inspired, when purposes align, and when hearts are genuinely cared for.

About Sheryl

Sheryl Driggers is a recognized keynote speaker and leadership coach renowned for her expertise in helping business owners forge purposeful, profitable, and joy-filled companies. With a bachelor's degree in business and marketing, Sheryl is not only a certified coach and trainer for the John Maxwell organization but also a Maxwell Certified Behavior Analysis Trainer.

She has spoken to thousands in leadership conferences and has worked with major corporations such as Nissan, Stellantis, CollisionRight, CARSTAR, and The Women's Industry Network. She has had the incredible opportunity to share the stage with best-selling author Chris Voss at the Disney Institute, and she speaks passionately about topics such as "Creating More Peace and More Profit" and "Finding Purpose Beyond Business," making her a sought-after speaker and thought leader in entrepreneurship.

Her profound impact on corporate culture has earned her features in prominent business magazines as well as the title of Culture Master on the cover of *FenderBender* magazine. She has been honored with the Most Influential Women Award from The Women's Industry Network and the Big M Courage Award for her upbeat and hopeful inspiration to others. Sheryl's insights into creating healthy team dynamics and impactful businesses are further shared through her contributions to the "Leadership" and "Customer Experience" columns of *ABRN* magazine, as well as several leadership podcasts.

As the author of the Weekly Devotionals for her church, she extends her influence to a broader audience, leading people to deepen their faith. Sheryl discusses themes of perseverance, the secrets of success for high-performing business owners, and finding her identity beyond a career in her relationship with Jesus. Sheryl's dedication to community service is evident through her founding of The James 215 Project, a nonprofit organization aiding those in need. She works to live out her life philosophy of caring for people and delivering excellence in every area of her life.

Sheryl cherishes time with her family, including her husband of twenty-four years, Jason, and their children, nineteen-year-old Barrett and eighteen-year-old Madison. They're often outdoors at racetracks, softball fields, or hunting expeditions.

Learn more at www.SherylDriggers.com.

CHAPTER 21

WHAT IS YOUR WHY?

Money as a Tool to Live Your Best Life

By Trey A. Novara

"Your grandmother had a stroke. She and your grandfather will be moving in with us so we can help take care of her."

As a twelve-year-old child, hearing my father deliver this news to my brother and me felt like an out-of-body experience. It was as if I were watching the whole scene unfold from across the room, and in that moment, my life forever changed.

My grandmother was now adjusting to the effects of the stroke— unable to walk, talk, or care for herself independently ever again. Both of my grandparents had worked hard their entire lives, and yet they were still ill-prepared for the overwhelming price tag that came with specialized care.

My family and I had just moved into a new house. Now my parents were choosing to make the difficult decision of adding onto our modest home and inviting my grandparents to live with us.

The financial strain that this put on my parents was notable. It was a harsh lesson in the unforgiving nature of life and a stark reminder of the importance of preparation.

This early experience was imprinted on my heart. It became the catalyst for my career path as a financial adviser. I wanted to empower and assist others to build a foundation that would withstand life's unpredictable storms.

My career began in the aftermath of the 2008 stock market crash. The Dow hit its lowest level of the crisis at 6,469 on March 6, 2009. I graduated college two months later.

Many of my friends had already graduated and moved to New York for positions in finance. One friend even landed a competitive spot at the revered firm Bear Stearns. Yet by the time he was ready to move, Bear Stearns was no more.

We all know that the stock market is a volatile entity. Some days it teases with the promise of glory, and on other days it casts an ominous shadow. Its inherent roller coaster quality creates a landscape where what goes up must come down—only to ascend once more. Despite the market's predictable rhythm, your brain does not allow you to compute this logic.

It cannot.

I see this time and time again. Human nature is to succumb to panic. Biology will always defy logic and throw us into the fight-or-flight mode—despite the data that proves a down market will not stay down forever.

As a financial adviser in an increasingly fearful world, I know that before I can persuade anyone to trust me with their hard-earned money, I must be a student of the discipline that impacts the decision-making process for every prospect with whom I come into contact: behavioral finance.

Behavioral finance combines elements of psychology and economics into an understanding of how individuals make financial decisions.

One key concept in behavioral finance is the recognition of cognitive biases that impact decision-making. For example, individuals may tend to hold losing investments for too long due to a fear of realizing losses, even when it might be economically rational to sell.

Looking at the physical response, when you become stressed, adrenaline—one of the fight-or-flight hormones—surges. The endocrine system then increases its production of steroid hormones to perpetuate the stress response all over the body. Essential brain functions are prioritized, and nonessential functions are affected by this chemical response.

If you are scared that you will lose your retirement savings because the stock market is going down, fear and stress response may take over and more critical thinking may not always take place.

Not a great formula to make decisions that will affect your future and your livelihood.

This is where I enter the chat—to help boost the critical thinking mechanisms that can be helpful in these circumstances.

I am not affected like you are by short-term losses in your retirement savings. Stress does not distort my ability to rationally analyze your situation. As a result, I can objectively see the very best course of action to ensure the highest probability of financial success.

This is why I can say with full confidence, for me, persuasion is a *service*.

On a deeper level, persuasion can become your purpose.

THE JOY OF OBSTACLES

> The obstacle in the path becomes the path. Never forget, within every obstacle is an opportunity to improve our condition.
>
> —RYAN HOLIDAY

I am an avid golfer.

Golf can be a maddening game, renowned for its ability to defy logic and frustrate even the most skilled players. No matter how meticulously you practice, how precisely you align your stance, or how perfectly you execute your swing, that tiny, stationary ball can still chart its own unpredictable course. Yet amid the exasperation, there is a peculiar joy to it all that golf enthusiasts come to embrace. We accept the unpredictability and call it the "rub of the green."

The financial world, much like the golf course, presents its own set of obstacles. As a financial adviser, convincing clients to trust me with their life savings requires not just financial acumen but also the ability to navigate the choppy waters of market fluctuations. I find myself in a perpetual persuasion game, urging clients to "stay the course" and resist the panic that often accompanies tumultuous market conditions.

My very first client was a schoolteacher named Sharon who made a very modest salary. I had two hurdles to overcome. The first being that I was twenty-five years old with no experience, and I needed her to trust me. The second is that she was convinced her small salary disqualified her from saving for retirement. I liked Sharon, and witnessing her fear of the future tugged at my heartstrings. I could clearly see a path she was unable to see. When I showed her the retirement plan I had designed, how she in fact *could* save money, and what she would end up with down the road, Sharon broke down in tears.

Just like in golf, I have learned to play through the obstacles and stay focused on the goal of helping my clients build secure futures. It requires me to regularly swing through the challenges, and by staying committed to the mission, the fairway of success awaits.

Up a Burn without Your Clubs

In 2022 I had the chance to travel to Scotland and attend the 150th playing of the Open Championship on the Old Course at St. Andrews Links. If you are not a golf nut like me, you may not be impressed, but if you are, then you understand the significance of my trip. The Open is a very big deal! To further invoke excitement, I had the opportunity to play the course the Monday following the Sunday finish. A true moment of a lifetime.

The only problem was that my golf clubs never made it across the pond.

Here I was at The Home of Golf, and my clubs were stuck in some cargo hold back in the States. I had two choices: not play or rent a set of incomplete clubs that were not fitted for me. Of course, I played. Only I chose to focus less on shooting my personal best and more on enjoying the walk, the company, and the chance to play the wonderful game. I truly relished walking the greens that the best in the world had walked only twenty-four hours prior.

PASSION IS THE OXYGEN OF PERSUASION

No matter your goal, conditions are never going to be perfect. You are going to hit resistance, the economy will dip, and there will be rainy seasons, but in those troublesome times passion will save you.

A while back I got a phone call. The man on the other end of the line was a bit shy at first. He was a pastor, his wife was a teacher, and money was tight. They were living in an RV trailer as they prepared to move into a new home, and while he knew he needed to start putting money aside for the future, he did not think he had enough money to get started.

I see this a lot. Far too often I encounter hardworking people who are doing their best but feel certain obstacles are too great to overcome, and they count themselves out.

"I have too many expenses."

"You probably only accept clients who make a certain amount of money, right?"

It always saddens me to think anyone feels disqualified from taking personal responsibility over their lives.

My parents were young when they started our family, and yet they found a way to make a good life for us. We were not wealthy, and our financial situation was made more precarious when my grandparents moved in with us—but we never went hungry.

Embedded in my memories is the profound lesson of self-responsibility, reminding me that if I was not actively doing something for myself, no one else would be doing it for me.

I remind my clients of that all the time. No one is saving money *for* you, so you better be saving it for yourself!

Back to the pastor—I knew I could help him. I believed with all my heart that with the right kind of plan we could secure a future for his family and restore his pride. However, I needed him to believe that too. That is where passion comes into play.

Passion serves as the magnetic force that draws other people into the orbit of your conviction. When you are truly passionate about something, you are naturally confident, which inspires trust, which makes anyone you are talking to more receptive to your message.

Not only that, but when you are hitting a wall (real or imagined), passion is the rocket fuel that keeps you going. In the realm of persuasion it is not just about presenting facts—it is about infusing the issue before you with the fire of your belief.

Inevitably, he did end up working with me, and together we built a rock-solid plan.

It is a good thing that we did.

As not long after we met, he was diagnosed with terminal cancer. The money generated from our plan was enough to pay for his funeral costs, pay for the new house he and his wife were building, and put their kids through college.

This world needs passionate people striving toward a meaningful purpose. When you have a clear mission, whether it is to persuade a prospect to join your team or enroll new stakeholders in your vision, bring your passion to the table. It is in that contagious spark of your enthusiasm that influence and persuasion naturally happen.

CHILDREN DO WHAT FEELS GOOD. ADULTS DEVISE A PLAN AND FOLLOW IT.

You may have been perfectly calm when you turned on your TV today.

But soon, after a few minutes into a foreboding news story about the economy, something will happen to your brain.

Your amygdala, the area of your brain that contributes to emotional processing, will send a distress signal to your hypothalamus. This area of the brain functions like a command center, sending directions to your nervous system that will help you prepare for the fight-or-flight response.

This is incredibly useful if you are being chased by a bear.

At this instant, the brain function that was meant to keep you alive is keeping you from making sound decisions.

Your brain does not distinguish between being stressed over the bear versus making a decision that is outside your comfort zone.

To your brain, stress is stress.

So let me put your mind at ease—a market fluctuation is not going to kill you.

The real threat to your well-being is *not* a dip in the market. The *real* threat is our very human tendency to allow external factors to throw us into a panic, which in turn causes us to sabotage very sound thinking and very worthy goals.

This is true of investment behavior, but it is also true of any other goal on earth. Anytime we are working toward something, we are going to hit resistance and roadblocks. Whether you are writing a book, starting a business, or saving for retirement, you must train yourself to make decisions that get you closer to your goal, rather than making decisions based on how you *feel*.

We feel uncomfortable, so we abandon the plan. We feel scared, so we abandon the plan.

When if we had just held out for a little longer, the atmosphere would have reset, and we may have struck gold.

LIFE IS NOT LEATHER-BOUND AND GOLD-LEAFED

When a client comes to meet with me at my office in Birmingham, Alabama, I work diligently to get to know them on a personal level first. I want to learn their deepest fears, their desires, and their hopes for the future. I research and run numbers and do everything I can to deliver a plan that will help them reach their goals.

I give that plan to the client on a piece of plain white paper. The plan is printed in black ink. There is nothing fancy or pretty about it. Even though the words and figures on that paper hold the key to their future, it is not leather-bound and gold-leafed because I know that in one year it will be outdated and in need of revision.

Financial planning is not a one-time thing. It is a lifelong pursuit full of twists and turns, ups and downs, and enough shifts to make you dizzy.

Life is the same way.

If you were able to persuade your team to work on a new and complicated project today, odds are that in a few weeks you will have to persuade them to pivot—and you will do so right before you go home to persuade your child to eat their vegetables and do their homework.

Our relationship with persuasion and influence is a lifelong pursuit that asks something new of us every single day.

The only constant in life is change. Babies will be born. Relationships change. There will be joy and challenges. You have two choices: Blame everything that goes wrong on the sand bunkers your golf ball keeps finding its way into, or adjust for your new condition and play the ball as it lies. Accept the rub of the green.

I hope you will think about that the next time you find your ball in a sand bunker in the form of red tape, a worthy adversary, or your own sophisticated brain threatening to derail you from what you could realize.

Return to the plan. Call on your passion to remind you of the destination you are pursuing.

Remember, persuasion is a service. Influence is a gift.

At some point, your unwavering commitment to "get your way" might just change someone's life, family, and home.

About Trey

Trey A. Novara, CFP®, AWMA®, is an award-winning practitioner in the financial services industry, where he currently owns and manages two companies. Trey became a CERTIFIED FINANCIAL PLANNER™ (CFP®) in 2014 and earned the Accredited Wealth Management Advisor (AWMA®) designation through the College for Financial Planning® in 2022. These designations require members to meet ongoing education requirements, adhere to a code of ethics, and demonstrate competency in the areas of wealth planning, risk management, retirement planning, investments, tax planning, and estate planning for high-net-worth individuals and families.

Trey takes immense pride in his ability to identify the best opportunities for his clients and determine how to maximize their success. He tailors plans specifically for each client while never neglecting peace of mind in the pursuit of pure performance metrics. As a fiduciary obligated to act in his clients' best interests, Trey simplifies complex issues by creating clarity and generating trust. Trey's mission is to put people, not institutions, in control of their own hard-earned money—allowing them to keep more of the money they make.

By regularly attending conferences and participating in continuing education, Trey advances his knowledge and capabilities, all while growing his own personal approach to successful wealth management. Trey's commitment to education ensures that he is always up to date on latest developments while providing his clients with the highest quality of service. He understands that his job is not just about managing wealth, but helping clients realize their dreams and accomplishing their goals.

Birmingham, Alabama, is where Trey calls home—along with his wife, son, and two dogs. As a philanthropic advocate for the city, Trey has held leadership positions in many community outreach programs and non-profit organizations. He is an active member of his church and enjoys his time fostering youth programs and participating in fundraising for a local child advocacy center and Folds of Honor. An avid sports fan, auto enthusiast, and golfer, during his free time Trey can be found cheering on his alma mater, the Auburn Tigers (War Eagle!), driving a vintage vehicle, working on his golf game, or traveling with his family.

To learn more about Trey, visit liveoakptrs.com or call 205-208-1716.

CHAPTER 22

HACKING INTO YOUR HIDDEN POTENTIAL

The Power of Leaning in to Adversity

By Alan Orlikoski

T he shrill ringing of the phone pierced through the quiet of the night, jolting me awake from sleep. I should be used to it by now. It happens every week. Yet my heart is still racing from the rude awakening when I reach for the receiver.

"You're needed in Sweden. Forty-eight hours."

My mind raced as I processed the mountains I would have to move to organize my life here while hurriedly preparing to travel to the other side of the world in just forty-eight hours to take lead on a crisis I currently knew nothing about.

That's the world of incident response. The details were always scant: another cybersecurity crisis, another race against time. Every week, for years, I would get a phone call requesting my immediate presence in another country to combat a security breach before it had time to wreak havoc on the business.

If it sounds dramatic, it was. Lives, jobs, and hundreds of millions of dollars hung in the balance, with thousands of people counting on me to fix the problem.

I am a cybersecurity and incident response expert. My journey in cybersecurity began in the United States Air Force. From developing globally recognized digital forensics tools such as CyLR, CDQR, and Skadi to leading incident response teams at major corporations, my career has been defined by a relentless pursuit of excellence.

But it's a tense world in which every second counts.

Those middle-of-the-night calls meant I was about to get on a plane and visit a CEO on the absolute worst day of their career.

Someone had hacked into their network. Data was being stolen. Money was being stolen. And the heads of the companies were crumbling from the pressure, painfully aware that their stakeholders, clients, and employees would all be affected if they didn't stop the bleeding in time.

That's where I come in.

I'd like to say I put on my superhero cape, swoop in, and restore order in no time at all, but it's never that simple. In fact, even though I am there to rescue them, I am often met with massive resistance.

Imagine dealing with someone who is already in full-blown panic and telling them they need to spend $300,000 in new security measures to retrieve the data and make sure it doesn't happen again.

When emotions are high, logic is low.

I must explain why they need to spend six figures on software and put the entire company offline for two weeks. I have to convince them to trust me, and that's not easy when so much money is at stake.

So, while I may be there in the capacity of a security expert, it's my persuasion skills that save the day.

DEFUSING A BOMB

I could see the vein throbbing on his forehead.

His nostrils flared, and through clenched teeth he asked me why the system I put in place was preventing him from sending an email to his most important client.

Hundreds of millions of dollars were on the line, and that email needed to go out *that day*.

He was a ticking time bomb.

One of the biggest mistakes someone in my position can make is to ask, "Why?"

Why does the email need to go out that day?

"Why" questions can make the other party feel defensive. In an agitated situation, "why" can feel like an interrogation, which leads to a defensive response.

I need this CEO to trust me, so I've got to be careful not to compound the already challenging atmosphere. I do that by empathizing.

I break out the active listening techniques I learned from Chris Voss. Active listening is a skill that transcends the negotiation room. I have used active listening to persuade an executive, connect with my wife, and parent my children.

It's a skill anyone can learn, and it involves offering open-ended prompts that begin with phrases such as, "It sounds like," or, "It seems that," which makes the other party feel that you have heard their dilemma and are at least attempting to understand the importance of the outcome.

It's one of the fastest ways to defuse a temper so true collaboration and constructive problem-solving can begin.

MALICIOUS INSIDER

"Please help. He's going to kill me," came the desperate voice on the other end of the phone. I could feel the color drain from my face as the seriousness of the situation sank in. This was not a routine negotiation. It was a matter of life and death.

I was a part of a highly skilled fraud team at the time, and the call had come into our customer success center. A customer had a knife to their neck, and the terms were clear: empty the bank account, or someone was going to die.

It sounds like the plot of a Tom Cruise movie, but you'd be surprised how often things like this happen. Public relations experts just make sure you never hear about it.

In situations like this I don't have time to question myself.

Every word, every second counts. And failure is not an option.

As you can imagine, with so much on the line, it's not uncommon for self-doubt and limiting beliefs to creep in, and if I'm not careful, my mind can become my worst enemy.

In cybersecurity, we use the phrase "malicious insider."

What that refers to is a person within a company who compromises the security of that company. It's tricky because a malicious insider typically has employee access, and because of that they pose a serious risk. Often they will steal or sell information and intentionally introduce vulnerabilities.

It's a terrible and exploitative attack from within.

For most of us the malicious insider lurking in our midst is our mind!

In an incident response, whether an innocent person is being threatened or a hacker just infiltrated sensitive data, I am called in to be the calm center of the raging storm.

It's up to me to locate the breach and defuse the panic with a clear and effective plan.

Can you imagine what might happen if I doubted myself? If I showed up scared? If I was too timid to make recommendations? If I let self-doubt cloud quick decision-making skills?

In this industry a confident and positive mindset is 80 percent of the job.

I have to be the one point of stability when everything is falling apart.

After twenty-four years in this business, I know how to tame my own mind and lead with authority, but years ago I struggled with it.

I hadn't studied the ways that tone of voice, cadence, and breathing mattered, and it hindered my ability to gain trust.

Even today, in my current position, there are aspects of our security program that I don't have twenty years of experience with, but I must trust in my own ability to lead.

If the customer isn't confident, they don't move forward with the security plan, and then they are left vulnerable. That means that my mindset is responsible for protecting every staff member, every customer, and all their families.

If I can't hold it together and empower a team to take the security measures they need to take, money is lost, jobs are lost, and lives are irreparably damaged.

Think about that the next time you're in a high-stakes situation and your inner critic starts shouting at you. It will work hard to make you believe you're not ready or can't handle it. It will remind you of that one time in third grade you screwed up, and if you let it, it will stop you from making the impact you need to make.

Remember that the voice you're hearing is nothing but a malicious insider. Escort it out of the building!

THE CHALLENGE THAT ROCKED MY WORLD...AND MADE ME A BETTER LEADER

Between 2019 and 2023 my world was rocked by my daughter's battle with mental health challenges, culminating in a dire need for specialized care that was not covered by insurance.

Even though we did everything we could to help her, every night, for two years, my wife and I went to bed knowing there was no guarantee our daughter would be alive in the morning.

It was gut-wrenching. This period required not only emotional resilience but also a strategic pivot in my career to secure the necessary resources for her treatment.

We were advised to place her into a treatment facility, so that's what we did. But none of it was covered by insurance.

I quickly took a position with Target because the signing bonus alone would completely cover the cost of her care. It was clear that while I had made the right decision for my daughter (and have never regretted that), I had backed myself into a corner I didn't want to be in.

Instead of stepping into the strategic leadership role I was promised (and more than qualified for), I was trapped in a position that pushed me to my limits.

It was a tactical leadership role that required a six-day work-week and eighty hours each week.

I should have known something was up when, on my first day, my new boss let me know it was his last day. The team was over-whelmed and overworked, and morale was low.

At this point in my career I was a fixer. I could see what needed to change, and I knew I could distribute the workload, solve the attrition problem, and do it all without sacrificing security.

My goal was to help. I realize now that I came in like a bull in a china shop.

After just a few weeks of being there, I was called into the office. "We're not sure you're a good culture fit."

What? I was just trying to help!

I knew that statement was a precursor to a termination, and I couldn't let that happen. If I got fired, I would have to return the signing bonus, and that money was already gone to pay for my daughter's treatment.

That's when I picked up a copy of Chris Voss' book *Never Split the Difference*. The book was more than a guide to negotiation; it was a beacon of hope, offering insights into human communication that resonated deeply with me. I dove into mastering these skills, applying them to navigate the complexities of my role at Target and the personal challenges I faced at home.

And one day it hit me. That team had been through a lot. They were scarred and fragile. They didn't need a bull. They needed a compassionate leader.

In my effort to enact quick change, I had come across as arrogant and critical.

I embarked on an apology tour and began practicing the tactics I was reading about.

It made a monumental difference in how the team received me. And I didn't get fired.

Have you ever heard the story about the fly who is desperately trying to get outside? He flies as hard as he can into the door again and again, so committed to getting through the closed door that he fails to notice the open window on the other side of the room.

Don't be the fly.

Had I stubbornly adhered to my way of doing things at Target, the result would have been disastrous for my family.

If you ever feel as if you're not getting anywhere with a certain situation or person, change the approach.

Find the window.

What It Really Takes to Succeed

Late 2022 and early 2023 brought the devastating loss of both my parents, adding to the emotional turmoil of the previous years. Rather than succumbing to despair, I channeled my grief into mastering communication techniques.

These skills proved invaluable as I navigated the tech industry's turbulent job market in 2023, characterized by widespread layoffs and unprecedented competition for cybersecurity positions.

After numerous applications I secured a role that represents the pinnacle of my career. As head of cybersecurity for Stream Data Centers, I am given a daily opportunity to apply the skills and lessons learned over the last twenty-plus years.

This role not only marks a high point in my professional journey but also embodies the culmination of a long and prosperous path of personal growth.

What I hope that anyone reading this remembers is that I wasn't born knowing how to lead tense situations or influence highly powerful people.

It's a skill set. Just like you can learn how to play guitar, you can learn the skills to persuasively communicate.

Skills are a lifeline that can anchor us. Unlike our emotions, which are fleeting, or even our intellect, which can fail us in a tense situation, skills are the tools in our toolbox that are always at our disposal once we've learned them.

I'm no smarter than you, no luckier than you, and no better-looking! All it really takes to succeed is a willingness to learn a new skill, practice that skill, and if you really want to make an impact, teach it to others too.

THE ANTIVIRUS SOFTWARE WE ALL NEED

For four years I couldn't walk.

I had degenerative disc disease that prevented me from standing for more than ten minutes at a time.

If I decided to test that limit, my legs would go numb and I'd fall over.

In January of 2024 I had surgery and can walk now, but for a long time I was severely limited by the disease. I know that had I not done the mindset work, that combination of my disability, my daughter's struggles, and the loss of my parents, all in quick succession, would have been unbearable.

If you think about it, cybersecurity provides a tidy analogy for the curveballs life throws at us.

Just as I might go into a system to deploy firewalls and encryption for the safeguarding of data, we must erect firewalls in our mind to protect ourselves.

Cultivating mental strength and resilience is one of the best measures you can take to protect yourself from any external threat.

The hackers will sneak in and try to derail you. They will look like negative self-talk and criticism. They will come in the form of challenging coworkers, broken-down cars, and unexpected losses.

Have your backup system ready!

Much like updating antivirus software to prevent a breach, continuing to fortify your own mind and skills is your most powerful weapon against anything life throws at you.

My journey through the worlds of cybersecurity and personal adversity has taught me the invaluable role that negotiation and communication play in all facets of life. The skills I've learned not only have transformed my approach to professional challenges but also have provided a framework for navigating the most difficult personal trials.

This narrative is a testament to the power of empathy, strategic communication, and resilience—principles that are as applicable in the boardroom as they are in your life.

About Alan

Alan Orlikoski is a distinguished cybersecurity expert with a profound impact across various sectors, including government, finance, and tech industries. His career began in the military, evolving through roles at prestigious organizations such as Booz Allen Hamilton, Mandiant, Hewlett Packard, Oracle, Target, Block, and Stream Data Centers, where he has consistently safeguarded critical information against evolving digital threats.

Alan is renowned for his development of open-source cybersecurity tools such as CyLR, CDQR, and Skadi, which have enabled and empowered a new generation of cybersecurity professionals. His contributions have earned him accolades, including teaching workshops at DEFCON and presenting at multiple SANS events, highlighting his role as a vanguard of cybersecurity innovation.

Beyond his technical mastery, Alan is committed to leadership through education, and mentoring a new generation of cybersecurity professionals. His effective communication skills bridge the gap between technical detail and strategic business needs, enhancing organizational resilience. His guidance has not only shaped security practices but also cultivated a culture of continual improvement and strategic foresight in the industry.

Alan enjoys mountain biking and family time with his wife and children. His journey from a serviceman to a cybersecurity luminary is a testament to his dedication to excellence and innovation.

For collaborations or to learn more about Alan's transformative approach to cybersecurity, leadership, and effective communication, visit orlikoski.com.

CHAPTER 23

TO INFLUENCE, DON'T TRUST YOUR MIND— TRUST YOUR GUT

By Pablo Linzoain

should never have come here…"

The cold English wind blew around me, a stark contrast to the heat rising in my cheeks. That's what happens when I get embarrassed.

I was born in Argentina but had traveled to England for what was supposed to be a three-month immersion into the English language while I continued my schooling. Having just arrived, I was eager to explore the area. That morning, I had decided to brave the cold and take the bus to Manchester.

"Eighty-seven cents?" I asked the bus driver.

"What?" he said in an annoyed tone.

"Eighty-seven cents?" I repeated, this time a little louder.

"Huh?" he chuckled. "What are you trying to say?" he replied condescendingly.

"Eighty-seven cents?"

"What's he saying?" he asked the guy sitting behind him, who only smirked and shrugged.

At this point I am painfully aware of the line forming behind me and the impatient stares from the people already on the bus, who were not at all happy with this delay.

"Eighty-seven cents? Is it?" In my head I was saying it clearly. I knew my English was far from clear, but I didn't think it was incomprehensible, and to be treated that way in front of all those people made me feel more like a scolded child than the grown man I was.

He shook his head again.

I could feel tears stinging my eyes. I turned and walked back home, defeated, angry, and ashamed that I wasn't even capable of boarding a bus in this new country.

I didn't try to take the bus the next day. I didn't go anywhere. I felt it was much less humiliating to just stay home and not speak at all.

I can't remember what finally pulled me out of that dark place, but I suddenly realized I could pay one pound and go anywhere on the bus route. "One pound" was easier to say than "eighty-seven cents." I made up my mind that the next day, I would just hand him one pound, get on the bus, and go where I wanted to go.

And that's what I did.

I trusted my gut, and as the bus pulled up, with the same guy in the driver's seat, I proudly held out my hand, clearly said, "One pound," and got on the bus. After a few weeks, he knew me and, I dare say, even liked me. I continued to overpay by thirteen cents every day, but I didn't care.

I went where I needed to go! Warren Buffett said, "Price is what you pay; value is what you get," and I got what I wanted.

Sure, I overpaid by a little, but I accomplished my goal, and the benefit that brought far outweighed the extra expense.

I've come a long way since those bus rides in England. Over the last twenty-five years I've worked in the high-stakes world of mergers and acquisitions, leading negotiations for some of the biggest companies in the world.

What I have learned over time is this: Trust your gut. We never know what the other side is going to bring to the table, so when preparation isn't possible, you need to use your gut and lead without fear.

I've learned that sometimes flexibility and focusing on what you want, even if you're overpaying, are keys to success.

COMPETITION VERSUS COLLABORATION

You could hear the yelling from ten houses down. Two sisters fighting over the last orange.

One claimed she saw it first.

The other claimed she should have it as the oldest.

Finally, unable to stand the drama any longer, the mother snatches the orange away from them and chops it in half.

One sister took her half, ate the orange pulp, and threw away the peels. The other sister took her half and used the peels to make a pie and threw out the pulp.

The moral of the story?

Their competitive spirits got the best of them, and they both got *less* than they could have had. Had they talked and collaborated, they would have learned that they each wanted a different part of the orange.

Their needs actually complemented one another, but they didn't know that. They had failed to demonstrate curiosity and empathy, the cornerstones of a successful collaboration.

I have won hundreds of negotiations just by finding out what the opposing party wanted and *why* they wanted it. But I wasn't always so wise!

Years ago at Harvard Law School a professor named Roger Fisher changed my life.

I had been working tirelessly on a dissertation about the cultural differences between the United States and Latin America. For two years I researched and labored, and when I proudly handed a draft to my professor, he said something I'll never forget.

"Pablo," he said kindly, "tell me one culture in the world that doesn't want to be loved."

I was stunned for a minute. What did love have to do with it? But I respected this man, so I answered.

"Every culture wants to be loved."

"Exactly," he said, "so why are you focusing on the differences? Focus on the similarities."

Two years of work was down the drain, but it was worth it. That conversation changed the course of my life. Humans tend to gravitate toward people who are similar. We are naturally attracted to people who remind us of ourselves.

After that conversation, I changed my perspective and studied to understand desires, insecurities, possibilities, and similarities. It is those universal threads connecting us all that help us build bridges to better communication and collaboration.

Professor Roger Fisher convinced me to not finish my PhD and focus on business instead.

He told me that the world needed people like me, people who were able to lead with strength but empathy. People who could foster collaboration over competition.

I love my work, but I am amazed at the way people are wired to compete without questioning the purpose. Sometimes the biggest obstacle to influence isn't the other side; it is our own mind. We are afraid to lose, so we hide information with our insecurity and don't connect with the other side because fear overprotects us.

We just want to be right.

Some negotiators come to the table with a number in mind, and they stubbornly adhere to it because they feel that any flexibility would mean they are losing control. Instead, we need to be rigid on the vision of what we want but flexible on details to get there.

In one particular negotiation, I offered *more* than the other party originally asked for, and they refused! They were so focused on holding their position, they weren't even hearing the higher offer.

The measure of intelligence is the ability to change.

—ALBERT EINSTEIN

They walked away with half the orange because they came to *talk* but not to *listen*. If they had just been willing to listen and collaborate, they would have heard me offer them the whole thing. Many times our insecurity forces us to shut down our listening. And that is a costly mistake!

PERCEPTION VERSUS REALITY

In negotiations power is *perceived*.

Every word from the speaker is filtered through the lens of the listener. That means that every word we hear, we run through an operating system in our minds that is powered by our beliefs, our experiences, and our biases.

We are constantly assessing power.

The slightest shift in perception can completely alter the trajectory of a negotiation. We walk in the room, and our minds immediately assign stereotypes to the people we see. For example, we see someone and label them as white, male, American, wealthy, powerful.

It's important to remember that while those labels might be true, they are irrelevant at the negotiation table.

Perception is not reality. And often perception is rooted in fear. The opposite of fear is *intuition*, that pulling energy to move forward with your ideas. Good negotiators possess intuition, outstanding listening skills, empathy, and street smarts—often more so than book smarts. They may not have advanced degrees on the wall, but their most reliable skill set is their ability to trust their gut as it helps them discern between perception and reality.

When faced with a life-threatening situation, complex thinking shuts down and our brains revert to their primitive ways of survival: fight, flight, or freeze. From this state of mind, we cease to apply higher executive reasoning. We simply act on instinct.

This is why it's so important to check your assumptions at the door and focus on facts.

Focusing on the evidence allows you to calculate the legitimacy of your thoughts and guts.

Years ago I was in a tense negotiation with a Chilean company. I could tell that the executive team was intimated by their American counterparts, whom they perceived as more powerful. I could tell their perception was diluting their position. When I spoke to them on the phone, they were sharp and confident. Yet in person, in front of the executive team, they were quiet, unsure that their ideas could hold up.

We did come to a deal, but I felt bad about it. They didn't trust their guts and let their biases scare them into staying quiet. The Chilean company could have asked for more had they not let their perception overshadow the reality.

When you don't trust your gut, it can prove very costly in negotiations.

SYMPATHY VERSUS EMPATHY

"My father is dead."

I was silent for a moment and felt terrible for the son who had delivered the news about his father's passing.

The man who died had a thriving business. His son would assume ownership, but without his father's guidance he was totally lost. That's why he called me. He wanted me to come on board for 45 percent equity and help him keep the business running.

I went on to make a series of terrible mistakes.

First, I didn't speak up during negotiations. I didn't want to appear insensitive during what was a sad time for him.

Secondly, I didn't heed the advice of my lawyer, who suggested I negotiate 51 percent equity, as I had all the expertise.

Third, I made the huge mistake of confusing sympathy with empathy.

It was there all along—that little nagging feeling that something was not right. You may have felt that, that tense feeling in your shoulders or the hair standing up at the nape of your neck. That's intuition. That small whisper in the back of your mind that says, "Hey, wait a minute. Are you sure about that?"

There were signs. The new owner had no background in finance, marketing, or sales, while I had decades of experience.

If I had truly led the situation and negotiated 51 percent control of the company, I could have saved myself fifteen years of stress and frustration.

And not just me; it affected many people. Everyone was affected—the board, the employees, revenue, and production—until he retired.

As soon as the previous owner retired, I doubled production in a matter of ten months.

The lesson learned: Be empathetic, not sympathetic.

If you allow your negotiation to be clouded by feeling sorry for someone, you may end up feeling sorry for yourself! Never confuse empathy with sympathy. While you can have sympathy for someone's situation, you can't bring sympathy into a negotiation with you. If you do, you will be able to convince yourself that doing the wrong thing for the "right" reason is OK.

Be assertive but empathetic, instead of sympathetic. Don't assume your sympathy will pay off in an investment.

ASSUME VERSUS ASK

A big reason we fear negotiation is being afraid of the unknown. We can't predict the result, and the ambiguity is scary.

You know what you want, you have your reason to need it, but you are afraid of what the other side wants and needs and how far they will go to "win."

When fear takes over, we tend to go quiet and rely on assumptions, which is a recipe for disaster!

A very wealthy friend of mine posted an ad on craigslist to sell an old 1985 luxury car. The interested buyer said that it was for his son and pointed out every flaw he could find because he wanted to see the price drop.

My friend didn't need the money, so he invited the man to make him an offer. Yet the man continued to point out flaws and make an argument for why the price should be lower. He was so keen on talking that he had missed the opportunity to name his price.

My friend eventually grew frustrated and told him the car was no longer for sale. The buyer had assumed my friend wouldn't budge on the price, instead of asking if he could pay the price he wanted.

If we make demands based on appearance, rumors, or preconceived notions, we risk missing the chance to get exactly what we want.

> It is wiser to find out than to suppose.
>
> —MARK TWAIN

Asking questions to identify the needs and challenges of the other side is vital. Most of the time we have no idea how they feel, or if they will be honest, or how willing they are to collaborate. Sure, we can take notice of their tone of voice, body language, and facial expressions, but we must go beyond that and ask questions. Because everybody "lies" or shares only the facts they think will help their case to win.

Ask deep questions. And when they answer, ask even more questions to get to the root of the truth.

Every day, deals are lost, relationships are broken, and countries go to war, all because of assumptions and insecurities of the negotiators.

If we stop at appearances and preconceived notions, we lose the upper hand. Famous twentieth-century scientist Bertrand Russell argued that appearance is what we gather from our senses, while reality is something we can never really know.

We can't possibly know what the other party is truly thinking and feeling unless we ask and observe. What we *see* is just a mask. We have to get curious and investigate what is behind the individuals' masks by questions rather than relying on stereotypes.

As leaders, we must be confident enough to break the assumption barrier and cultivate deeper exploration.

FINAL THOUGHTS...

One final thing to remember is that in any situation that requires negotiation, most of the time we all want the same thing—a peaceful and mutually beneficial resolution.

If you commit to approaching every situation with a goal to

cooperate rather than compete, you will find yourself on the successful side of the negotiation process.

Be flexible and trust your gut.

Never be your own obstacle.

And always use empathy in your search for the truth.

About Pablo

Amid a landscape fraught with high-stakes business situations, Pablo Linzoain stands as a preeminent figure in the realm of negotiation, boasting a comprehensive international portfolio in successful conflict resolution management.

Recognizing persistent challenges in reaching agreements, Linzoain identifies systemic flaws as the crux of recurring issues rather than deficiencies in individual stakeholders. With over three decades of negotiation expertise, he has counseled numerous executives and corporate leaders across diverse geographies, including the US, Canada, Spain, Japan, Russia, and much of Latin America. Linzoain's consultancy endeavors have encompassed collaborations with prominent corporations such as BBVA, U. S. Steel, Heinz, and the University of Pittsburgh Medical Center.

Adept at leading intricate negotiation concepts, Linzoain's pedagogical approach simplifies complexities to expedite mutual understanding and collaboration. A perpetually evolving scholar, he holds certificates from esteemed institutions including The Business School of Manchester Metropolitan, MIT, and Harvard Law School's Dispute Resolution, Mediation, and Participatory Processes program.

As the founder and CEO of the Instituto de Negociación, established in 2016, Linzoain endeavors to furnish advanced negotiation training and coursework.

If you're having trouble reaching agreements, the problem isn't you. The problem is your system. Linzoain's brainchild, the Empathic Persuasive Story method, represents a sophisticated technical and methodological formula comprising seven foundational principles pivotal in conflict resolution. This methodology imparts bespoke strategies and techniques to harmonize disparate perspectives, evidenced by its successful implementation across varied contexts.

Acknowledging that adept negotiation transcends mere cognitive prowess, Linzoain emphasizes the significance of behavioral dynamics in fostering productive business relationships. His Empathic Persuasive Story method serves as a blueprint for individuals seeking to fortify their negotiating prowess, enrich interpersonal relations, broaden their appreciation of diverse viewpoints, and efficaciously navigate conflicts.

The main reason people struggle with negotiations is that they have spent years in school but learned nothing about empathy and relationships. The result is that people learn to only compete—and never learn to cooperate and influence.

Linzoain is steadfast in his mission to instill a deeper understanding of human dynamics throughout the negotiation continuum, thereby fostering cooperative interactions and positive outcomes. By imparting invaluable skills, he endeavors to cultivate a future marked by harmonious relations and collaborative endeavors.

Connect with Pablo at www.linzoain.com.

CHAPTER 24

TAPPING INTO YOUR SUPERPOWERS

The Keys to Influence and Impact

By Deepthi Barrett

f you look up the definition of the word *invisible*, here is what you will find:

in·vis·i·ble

a. Incapable of being seen

b. Not openly acknowledged

c. Of such small size as to be hardly noticeable

All these definitions of the word indicate an inherent quality on the part of whatever is being described as "invisible."

What I found to be true at a very early age, however, is that one can be in the room, and have earned the right to be there, and still be utterly invisible.

Outside in the hallway I could hear the chatter of the boys. I was enrolled in a summer program to learn advanced middle school math and science, and this was the first day.

I arrived early and sat at a desk. As the boys filed in, their chatter stopped, and every one of them sat on the other side of the classroom. I hoped at least one more girl would show up, but that didn't happen.

During the session the teacher faced the boys' side of the

classroom the entire time. It was intimidating to ask questions in that environment—first, it was advanced topics that I had no idea about; second, it was clear that there was implicit acknowledgment from the teacher that I wasn't going to understand it anyway.

Discomfort was tempting me to leave, but my desire to learn was stronger, so I put one foot in front of the other and made it through.

It was clear that the teacher had no idea what to do with me.

That summer, I became acutely aware of the challenges I would face as a girl in the world of science and math.

This was a scenario that would repeat multiple times in my life as I navigated my education and the workforce. I would be the only woman in certain classes, the only woman in certain networking groups, and eventually, the only woman in the C-Suite.

It was challenging, but over time something came alive in me, a spark of defiance that refused to be ignored. "Just watch me." I would show everyone that I was a powerful force to be reckoned with.

I would do it by learning to harness my own superpowers. And you can too.

The Superpowers of Influence

It doesn't matter if you're a man or woman, or black or white or Indian. It doesn't matter if you were born into poverty or into a gilded mansion.

Everyone has access to superpowers.

What I have found in my twenty years' experience as a data scientist for major corporations is that influence is everything. If you can master the art of influence, you can lead with authority, move the needle, and make sure you are never invisible again!

I worked for years as a consultant but decided a couple of years ago to take a permanent position with an energy company. As a consultant, you make a recommendation and go on your way. I was eager to see my recommendations in action and follow their trajectory all the way to the end. This company seemed like a good fit, and I believed in the industry. After all, the company powered gas and electricity. We are the lifeline to every household! I felt purpose in that.

On my first day it was very apparent that my team was not well liked. I could immediately see why. There was an air of awkwardness in every interaction, and recommendations were not well received. It would take time to investigate the reason for this, but once I figured it out, I realized that the solution for this team was the same solution I had used myself to overcome every obstacle that came my way.

Superpowers...

And more specifically, the superpowers of influence. There are four of them, and whether you're navigating the choppy waters of parenthood or the high-stakes world of business, understanding how to use them will determine whether you succeed or fail in your missions!

THE FIRST SUPERPOWER OF INFLUENCE: EMPATHY

Have you ever tried to get face time with someone whose problem you were trying to solve but found that they wouldn't give you the time of day?

That's the exact vibe I was met with when I first landed this role.

I was there to help, and yet no one wanted to talk to me. In their eyes I was an outsider. In their eyes I didn't know anything about the energy industry, and they weren't about to listen to me or let me waste their time. They saw me as an arrogant brainiac, there to inconvenience them.

It was mind-blowing.

How did we get here? How did my team, which provides vital data that keeps the company running, become the black sheep of the organization?

After a few weeks of observation I had my answer.

What I noticed was that the data team was presenting the data solutions. Sounds correct, but presenting data solutions to other teams in the company is the same as handing a book written in German to a person who only reads English!

The business side had no idea what the figures meant, which made our work irrelevant in their eyes.

They couldn't use what they didn't understand, so my team was useless to them.

My team was not practicing empathy. What we needed to do was put ourselves in the shoes of the other divisions and get curious about their goals. We also needed to stop presenting the facts and instead explain *how* the facts would help them reach those goals.

Furthermore, when an employee in the business division *did* ask a question, the data team took it as an insult! How dare anyone question our expertise? After years of bad blood between departments, there was a misconception that the business side was asking questions to challenge when in reality they were asking questions to better understand.

We shifted our approach and infused empathy into our interactions, and within six months, the same people who didn't even want to meet me were my team's biggest advocates!

THE SECOND SUPERPOWER OF INFLUENCE: CONFIDENCE

My father was a captain on oil tankers. That meant that he was away for four to six months at a time, leaving my mom as the primary caregiver for my brother and me.

My parents were building a home at the time, which meant that contractors were coming and going every day. Cultural norms in India dictate that the man of the house would normally act as project manager for something like this, but my dad was not there, which meant that my mom would have to fill those shoes.

I remember watching as she led this project, speaking with authority and mobilizing the construction team into action. I remember asking her how she knew so much about building a house to which she replied, "I don't know anything about building a house. I'm learning it by doing it."

My mother taught me an important lesson that day. Never let not knowing how to do something stop you from doing it!

No one in my extended family agreed with my father's decision to send me to America for undergrad. The idea of a young Indian girl, alone in a foreign country was too much for my relatives to imagine. They tried to persuade my father with gloomy predictions of financial ruin and other dangers waiting for me, but my father believed in me.

He refused to be swayed by patriarchal norms and his faith in me fueled my determination.

There I was, a young girl who had never gone anywhere on her own, embarking on a journey to start a new life in America. My luggage wasn't the only heavy thing I was carrying. I was carrying the weight of their sacrifice and of my own limiting beliefs.

I knew if I had any chance of succeeding, or even surviving, on my own, I would need to ditch the baggage of self-doubt and fast!

A tool I learned back then that I still use today is that questions are a bridge to confidence.

Ask questions!

If you don't know something, ask.

If you want to take a conversation deeper, ask.

If you want to find out what motivates the person on the other side of the negotiation table, *ask*!

Questions are doorways to information, and information is the bridge to confidence.

That's true whether you're leading a business interaction, working with a team, or trying to find your way as a young girl in a new country.

When everything is challenging, confusing or unclear, questions become a life raft that pulls you to shore.

THE THIRD SUPERPOWER: CURIOSITY

Something happens when you fight your whole life to be seen and taken seriously.

You run the risk of being a know-it-all!

This is something I see in business interactions all the time. Both teams have an agenda, and both are under the mistaken assumption that if they just talk more they will "win." What should be a collaboration turns into a contest to see who can use the biggest words, who has the fastest retorts and which side brings the most evidence.

In these cases both sides are desperate to show how much they *know.*

Years ago, as a grad student in a research lab I would tag along with my professor to meetings with the stakeholders of projects we were working on.

I knew the facets of our projects inside and out.

When the stakeholders asked questions, my professor would be silent. I'd be sitting on my hands and biting my tongue, trying to keep myself from shooting my hand in the air and yelling, "I know all these answers!"

Yet instead of answering their question, he would ask them one in return.

I learned in that situation that we can demonstrate our expertise by practicing quiet discernment and curiosity.

Allow some pause. Consider the question being asked, be curious and ask a countering question to get just a little more information. And pause again. I have studied human behavior for years and what I have found is that humans struggle with quiet.

If there is a pause, humans are wired to fill that pause. If you're in a high stakes discussion, go quiet! In that moment, the other side will almost always fill the silence by continuing to talk. The more they talk, the more information you gain to craft your response.

THE FOURTH SUPERPOWER: INTUITION

I couldn't sleep a wink. For days my mind would buzz in the middle of the night, my brain working overtime to find solutions for the problems at work. I would get out of bed to write down ideas and stay awake until morning. It was exhausting to be always "on" and running at a hundred miles per hour.

It wasn't until it started affecting my family that I realized I needed help.

I know now that what I was experiencing is something thousands of people experience every day: burnout!

My intuition had been whispering to me for months that something needed to change, but I had work to do. So I did what many busy people do. I quieted my own voice.

My intuition got louder, and still I trudged on, working long hours on little sleep.

You can only ignore your own voice for so long before that whisper becomes a scream!

Intuition is perhaps one of the most powerful superpowers in your arsenal.

It defies logic, and its wisdom extends beyond the edges of your textbook knowledge.

It's the voice of reason that cries for rest when the calendar is packed.

It's the voice of curiosity that prompts you to ask questions when your colleague seems to be shutting down a conversation.

You see we have many inner voices. Some of our voices are helpers, some are critics.

My inner critics were *loud*, echoing the sentiments of everyone who had ever doubted me.

"If I rest, I'll fall behind."

"If I don't hit the target, they'll think I'm not capable."

Growing up, I had a lot to prove. I set very high expectations for myself. I worked extra hard, and when deadlines were approaching, I doubled down and worked more. That turned out to be a good strategy for navigating a male-dominated world and building a career for myself.

What I discovered when burnout hit, however, was that the tools that had propelled me to the top of my industry were now the same tools that were wreaking havoc. My allies had become my enemies!

I was trapped in this cycle of hustle and exhaustion.

I embarked on a journey of mindfulness, connected with other women leaders for support and learned to listen to the voice of my own intuition again.

I thought about all the times my intuition had guided me. After all, when you have no answers and no roadmap, you still have intuition to turn to.

I used my intuition to chart my course in a new country. I used it when I was deciding what job would be the best fit. I used it when it was time to ask for help with my burnout. I use my intuition every day to try to read between the lines in business conversations.

But you can't hear the guidance of your intuition if it is drowned out by the chatter of your inner critic.

I encourage you to adopt the habit of pressing pause!

If you're feeling out of alignment, if an opposing team is asking challenging questions, if you have an important decision to make, press pause. In that pause, ask your intuition what to do next.

It will always have a suggestion. Your challenge is to commit yourself to following it.

TAKE YOUR PLACE

I grew up in India, watching American TV shows and listening to American music. But consuming American culture and living in America are two different things.

In India, seniority is very important, so I remember an incident that shocked me! I was in my fourth year of college and decided to visit some student organizations. I was surprised to find that a few of them had a freshman as president!

It never occurred to me to run for president of any of these clubs as freshman. I didn't even think it was an option. But then it hit me.

What a gift.

We live in a world now in which your highest aspirations don't require a permission slip. In fact, few paths beyond education even have prerequisites.

Whatever it is we want, we can have it.

Whatever role we want to play, we can play it.

We simply must tap into the storehouse inside of us that holds what we need to succeed: the courage to begin, the clarity to choose, and of course, the willingness to tap into the tools that will not let you down...

The superpowers of influence.

About Deepthi

Deepthi is a director of digital products at National Grid. She oversees a comprehensive portfolio aimed at managing solar, battery, and electric vehicle infrastructure on the power grid. Her strategic leadership and keen understanding of customer needs have led to the development of cutting-edge solutions that drive clean energy goals and deliver tangible business impacts. With a strong background in advanced data analytics, Deepthi has a proven track record of developing innovative solutions that drive efficiencies and generate substantial savings.

Before her role at National Grid, Deepthi held positions at consulting firms, where she led the development of analytical models to improve efficiencies for financial and pharmaceutical industries.

In addition to her professional endeavors, Deepthi is an advocate for education and innovation. As the founder of Spark EdTech, she developed educational games and programs, impacting hundreds of students in India and the US.

Deepthi holds a master of science in systems engineering from the University of Pennsylvania and a bachelor of science in electrical engineering from Purdue University. Follow Deepthi on LinkedIn to stay updated on her latest insights, projects, and speaking engagements: www. linkedin.com/in/dchandra.

CHAPTER 25

THE POWER OF TRUSTING YOUR INNER COMPASS

By Renetta Cheston

FROM BREAKING UP TO BREAKING THROUGH

The tears stung in my eyes, and it occurred to me that I was holding my breath.

Another breakup. Another broken heart. Here I was again in this all-too-familiar place, being hit by the flying debris of someone else's rage. Here I was again stepping over the broken shards of another shattered hope.

I seemed to be caught in this endless cycle of love and disappointment, and each time, the storm was more and more severe.

As I stood there processing this fresh ending, I felt the weight of a thousand memories pressing down on me, and I couldn't help but whisper over and over, "Why me?"

I watched as the montage played in my mind, showing me pictures of myself as a child being beaten, kicked, burned by an iron, berated, while my brother and sister were treated with kindness.

The movie screen played in my head, flashing images of brutal assaults, completely shocking and unprovoked and delivered by people who were supposed to protect me.

I could still feel the sting of the slaps. I could still hear the cruel taunts and my family's words playing on repeat in my head, "You don't belong here."

For decades I carried that story—that I didn't belong anywhere, that I was different and therefore bad, that I would never be good enough.

I went to bed that night numb and slept deeply, not because I was tired but because at least in sleep I could temporarily escape the pain.

When I woke up, I expected to be hit with the reality of the events that had occurred the day before. I expected to feel the pain and sadness, but instead, I felt strong.

A new and sacred fire surged through me, and like a switch had been flipped, I suddenly understood.

I didn't belong here, because I was a kind heart in a merciless world. I wasn't wrong. *They* were. I wasn't ugly. *Their* hearts were ugly.

With each moment, the clouds of long-standing sorrow dissipated, and in their place was a profound certainty of who I was, a sense of self-assuredness that had always eluded me.

The light of *my* truth burned bright with sudden clarity.

I *did* belong here. I was sent here to lead. And I *was* different.

Because while everyone around me was serving themselves, I was on a mission for God.

Today I coach my clients to practice the steps I have found to be the bedrock of a good life, one that is meaningful, impactful, and full of joy.

Feel your feelings.

Believe the signs.

Choose your story.

And trust yourself.

Feel the Feelings

Today I am an entrepreneur, a best-selling author, the CEO of a nonprofit, a pastor, and a life coach.

But I couldn't be good at any of those things if I hadn't walked through the fire and felt the burn!

I had to feel the rage, the confusion, the pain, and anguish before I could transmute those feelings into lessons and those lessons into love.

For me, influence is now a service. I exist to have influence on people so they can live the life God had planned for them. The very first thing I teach them is to feel their feelings.

Feelings hold valuable information and are the foundation of our values. Feelings are God's guidance and the basis of our inherent decision-making framework.

Everything begins and ends with feeling.

But human beings are tough! We are wired to resist.

When I am ministering and coaching people to practice feeling, which should come naturally, I'm amazed at how well we have trained ourselves to push down our emotions, to quiet them, to pretend they don't exist at all.

This might be useful on the front lines of war, but in life, in the home, and in the workplace, that unwillingness to feel wreaks havoc.

Have you ever witnessed someone in a leadership role throwing a tantrum, intimidating their employees into submission, and stomping around the office, giving orders and making demands? What you're witnessing are unprocessed emotions from an inner child who needs a hug!

You can't be in leadership and not deal with your demons, or the personnel who work under you will be exhausted trying to keep up.

You cannot parent effectively if you don't process your feelings, because your anger about an argument with your spouse will at some point land on your child.

Feelings need to *go* somewhere, and if we don't process and release them, we run the risk of becoming a source of negative influence for the people around us.

You see, influence isn't just what you do or what you say; it's how your emotions and the resulting energy you carry affect other people.

So, if you truly want to make an impact, you've got to make friends with feeling.

Sometimes it's as simple as taking a moment to ask yourself,

"Why do I feel so angry? Why am I so tired?" and then pausing to listen for the response from within. When you can define and label the source of your feelings, you are one step closer to letting them go.

When I think back to what I went through, I realize that the patterns of abuse and disappointment played on repeat because I wasn't processing my feelings around them. I was going numb, hoarding those feelings, my arms holding tight to years and years of resentment.

God wanted me to deal with my feelings and release them to make room for what he was sending.

Whatever you're holding on to, remember, you can't pick up anything good while your arms are still holding mountains of grief and bitterness.

Feelings need to move through you. Feel the weight of your emotions in the palm of your hand.

And then, at long last, let them go so your arms can pick up what is *truly* meant for you.

Nothing Is a Coincidence

Have you ever had a dream that was so vivid, so jarring that you woke up and remembered every single detail?

If you're like most people, when this happens, you take a moment to think about it, say to yourself, "Hmmm, that was strange," and then forget all about it and go about your day.

I used to do that too, until I realized that absolutely nothing is a coincidence.

I remember sitting at my desk one morning after a dream like that. In that dream I was very clearly shown that I was adopted. The scene was clear as day, and in the dream I was stoic, accepting, as though it made total sense. I was troubled by it. I tried to work, tried to push it out of my mind, and made a silent prayer, asking God why this random dream was weighing so heavily on me. In an effort to distract myself, I clicked on a random YouTube video. The headline of that video was this:

"The Dream You Had Last Night Was Real."

I was stunned...and I knew it was true.

Albert Einstein said, "There are two ways to live your life. One is as though nothing is a miracle. The other is as though everything is a miracle."

I realized in that moment how often we have a choice and make the less miraculous one.

How often have you asked for a sign, received one, and ignored it completely, dismissing it as sheer coincidence?

Signs are God's method of persuasion!

Signs and dreams are not random. They are a Divine communication.

But we talk ourselves out of faith and into skepticism.

We persuade ourselves to look away from the very influence we seek!

Have you done that? Have you ever felt something so deeply but persuaded yourself to believe that you heard nothing, that you saw nothing, and that it meant nothing?

If so, you are not alone. You see, we all have an ego, and that ego is there to help us make sense of the world.

Yet in an effort to make logical sense, it drowns out Divine guidance...and steers us far away from the path we are meant to walk.

Believe the signs. Pay attention to your dreams.

Every nudge that you notice is a well-placed piece of advice from a guardian angel who wants to see you win!

CHOOSE YOUR STORY

As I stumbled back toward the military base, my ears were still ringing from the music and the joyful noise of my friends' voices.

I was on a deployment in Panama, and it was my twenty-first birthday. I had never been drunk before, but my friends were determined to help me celebrate this milestone. Now, dizzy and tired, I walked clumsily around the NCO Club, my friends nowhere to be found, and ran smack into an officer. I felt relieved to have run into someone I could trust to get me to my bed safely.

What he did instead was rape me.

I knew it was coming. My throat tightened, and my voice, though hoarse from the night out, was very clearly saying, "No."

When it was over, I felt a searing pain of betrayal, but I also knew in that moment that not a single person would take my side in this.

And they didn't. Instead, they sent me home.

I had learned so much about myself overseas and become self-reliant in a way that made me proud. Yet all the way across the world, the same story had followed me. I had found myself in the same plot, occupying the same role...

Victim.

It wasn't the first time, and it wouldn't be the last. I remember wondering how many oceans I had to cross to distance myself from the shackles of my past.

It would be years later before I would awaken to the truth.

Everything that happens, happens *for* us, not *to* us.

All our ups and downs, all our joys and heartaches, are just chapters in our stories. Those chapters make up our Hero's Journey.

I don't know that there is anything more powerfully persuasive than the Hero's Journey. It's a story we all love and relate to.

It starts with a calling to leave behind what we know so we can embark on an adventure, one that is wrought with obstacles and villains but ultimately leads us to our destiny!

Nearly every story we read or blockbuster movie we watch is based on this same narrative structure. But the Hero's Journey is not fictional.

Every one of us is on that same kind of journey.

We just stay stuck in the middle of the story! We forget that we are the Hero and identify too heavily with the obstacles and "bad guys."

I don't know about you, but I like a happy ending. I don't want to read a story that allows the bad guy to take the lead and win in the end.

I realized as I got older that I can step out of any role in any story that is incongruent with how I want to live and serve.

I realized I had spent my whole life in other people's stories, sharing other people's pain, suffering the brunt of other people's trauma.

If someone runs by you with a full glass of water, some of it is bound to splash onto you.

That's what was happening. I had stayed in close orbit to too many hurt people, and their pain spilled over onto me.

Where in your life are you being influenced by other people's stories, stories that have nothing to do with who you are and how you want to live?

How many times have you allowed someone else to convince you that you weren't good enough and would never succeed?

I invite you on this day to persuade *yourself* to step away from anyone who is distracting you from the depth and beauty of your own calling.

Persuade *yourself* to release anything working against the sacred pull of your purpose here on earth.

Persuade *yourself* to step into a new story, with dynamic characters, exciting plot twists, and fairy-tale endings.

A story directed and produced by you but fully funded and backed by God!

When You Can't Trust Anyone, Trust Yourself

As I stepped into the sanctuary, I felt a sense of pending relief.

Finally, I was going to tell my pastor about the abuse I was experiencing at home. Finally, an adult I trusted was going to step in to help.

The familiar scent of burning candles grew stronger as I stepped into his office. I spilled every horrible detail. When I finished speaking, I waited for him to comfort me. I waited to see compassion on his face.

What happened instead was a nightmare.

He walked out and told everyone within earshot that I was a troubled girl with a demon inside me. "Whatever you hear, know that I am just helping to expel these demons from her body and soul."

You can imagine what happened next. I left there a different person, my innocence gone, my trust shattered.

I decided at that moment that I would never trust anyone other than myself.

I would ask *myself* what to do next. I would ask *myself* why I felt the way I felt. I would ask *myself* for guidance.

What I know now is that the inner voice I was finally choosing to listen to is the voice of God!

Whatever you believe, the whispers of your instincts and intuition are the voice of a higher power, one that sees far beyond the limits of our jaded human perception.

Trust it.

Trust it when it's telling you to take action. Trust it when it's telling you to change course.

How many times do we hear our intuition tell us to move on, but we cling. We bang on closed doors. We fight to retrieve what is *meant* to be lost.

That human tendency to resist inner guidance lands us on a merry-go-round of repeated painful lessons.

I can almost picture God throwing his hands up in frustration, yelling, "Don't fight! It's me! I'm trying to help you! Just go with it and let me handle it, for crying out loud!"

Our intuition tries to speak, but what it's saying goes against our plan, our vision, or our timeline, so we push it aside.

Maybe your intuition is telling you to follow an idea that the rest of the team doesn't believe in.

That's when it's most important to stand ten toes deep in your *own* belief!

It's never easy to lead with intuition. It will ask you to take a stand for things that only you can see.

But the people who are willing to do just that, no matter how crazy they sound, are the people who end up having the most impact and ultimately changing the world.

About Renetta

Renetta Cheston is not just the author of *In the Garden with the Father: Understanding True Intimacy*, but a beacon of resilience and empowerment in her own right. A lifetime member of the Worldwide Women's Association, Renetta's journey is a testament to the power of faith, courage, and unwavering determination.

As a mother, grandmother, and jack-of-all-trades, Renetta recently experienced life-altering events that prompted her to seize the opportunity for a fresh start. Despite the challenges, she embraced the chance to rewrite her story, pursuing her dreams with relentless fervor.

Previously thriving as a licensed massage therapist and holistic practitioner in Atlanta, Georgia, Renetta's life took a sudden turn, forcing her to pivot and embark on a new chapter. It has been a daunting journey marked by uncertainty, but Renetta approached it with resilience and a steadfast belief in God.

Renetta advocates for others to take control of their lives and transform them, one mindset at a time. Drawing from her own experiences of ups and downs, she inspires through her blogs, demonstrating that restarting life is possible with hard work and determination.

A serial entrepreneur fighting for her freedom, Renetta is committed to living life on her own terms. Through her journey of self-discovery she has uncovered her true, authentic self and encourages others to do the same. Renetta believes that life is meant to be lived authentically, free from the constraints of societal expectations.

Her dream is to make a global impact by organizing nonprofits across various locations, spanning cities, states, and countries. Additionally, she is dedicated to supporting women who may have lost their path along the way.

Renetta Cheston's story is one of resilience, faith, and the power of embracing change. With unwavering determination and trust in God, she continues to inspire others to take control of their lives and pursue their dreams with courage and conviction.

www.ingramcontent.com/pod-product-compliance
Lightning Source LLC
Chambersburg PA
CBHW070703190326
41458CB00046B/6826/J